der
can
an
.d
e y
ca

Lea

HOW TO LOSE
A COUNTRY

ECE TEMELKURAN

How to Lose a Country

The Seven Steps from Democracy to Dictatorship

4th ESTATE • *London*

For Umut.
His name means 'hope' in my mother tongue.

4th Estate
An imprint of HarperCollins*Publishers*
1 London Bridge Street
London SE1 9GF

www.4thEstate.co.uk

First published in Great Britain in 2019 by 4th Estate

Copyright © Ece Temelkuran 2019

1

Ece Temelkuran asserts the moral right to be identified
as the author of this work in accordance with the
Copyright, Designs and Patents Act 1988

A catalogue record for this book is
available from the British Library

HB ISBN 978-0-00-829401-4
TPB ISBN 978-0-00-829635-3

Printed and bound in Great Britain by
CPI Group (UK) Ltd, Croydon, CR0 4YY

MIX
Paper from
responsible sources
FSC
www.fsc.org   FSC™ C007454

This book is produced from independently certified FSC paper
to ensure responsible forest management.

For more information visit: www.harpercollins.co.uk/green

Contents

INTRODUCTION

What Can I Do for You?

The fighter jets are breaking the dark sky into giant geometric pieces as if the air were a solid object. It's 15 July 2016; the night of the attempted coup in Turkey. I am piling pillows up against the trembling windows. I guess they've just dropped a bomb on the bridge, but I can't see any fire. People are talking on social media about the bombardment of the Parliament Building. 'Is this it?' I ask myself. 'Is tonight the Reichstag fire for what remains of Turkish democracy and my country?'

On TV, a few dozen soldiers are barricading the Bosporus bridge, shouting at the startled civilians: 'Go home! This is a military takeover!'

Despite their huge guns, some of the soldiers are clearly terrified, and all of them look lost. The TV says it's a military takeover, but this is not a coup as we know it. Coups usually wear a poker face – there's no hustling or negotiating, and certainly no hesitation when it comes to using the heavy weaponry. The absurdity of the situation sees sarcasm kick in on social media. This kind of humour is not necessarily aiming for laughter; it's more of a contest in bitter irony, which seems normal only to those engaged in it. The jokes mostly concern the idea that this is a staged act to legitimise the presidential system – rather than the parliamentary one – that President Recep Tayyip Erdoğan has long been asking for, a change that would hand him even more power than he already has as the *de facto* sole ruler of the country.

The dark humour disappears as the skies over Istanbul and Ankara become busy hives of fighter jets. We are learning the language of war in real time. What I'd thought was a bomb was actually a sonic boom – the blast-like sound fighter jets make when they break the sound barrier. This is the proper terminology for the air breaking into giant pieces and raining down on us as fear: fear of realising that before the sun rises we might lose our country.

People in the capital city of Ankara are now trying to differentiate between sonic booms and the sound of real bombs hitting Parliament and the intelligence service headquarters. The catastrophe unfolding in front of our eyes is constantly blurred by the absurdity of the news reports on our screens. Live on air, MPs are running around Parliament trying to find the long-forgotten air-raid shelter, and when they finally do locate it, nobody can find the keys, while outside in the streets people dressed in their pyjamas are kicking tanks, cigarettes in their mouths, and shouting at the jets.

A communications explosion is occurring on our TV screens, and many of us know that this is very much not normal. Turkey's recent history has taught us that a coup starts with the army taking politicians into custody and shutting down news sources. Also, coups tend to happen in the early hours of the morning, not during television prime time. In this meticulously televised coup, government representatives appear across TV channels all night long, calling on the people to take to the streets and oppose the army's attempted takeover. The internet does not slow down in the way it usually does whenever something occurs to challenge the government; on the contrary, it's faster than ever. Even so, the speed and intensity of the night's events do not allow the sceptics to properly process these strange details.

Erdoğan communicates using FaceTime, with his messages broadcast on CNN Turk. He calls everyone out into the city centres. Like most people, I do not anticipate the government's supporters taking to the streets to confront the military. Since the founding of the modern Turkish republic in 1923, under Kemal Atatürk, the army has traditionally been the most respected institution in the country, if not the most feared. But apparently much has changed since the last military coup in 1980, when it was the leftists who resisted and were imprisoned and tortured; the president's call resonates with thousands.

In no time the TV screens are showing the young, terrified soldiers being beaten and strangled to death by this mob. And that is when the never-ending *sela* from all the minarets in the country begins. *Sela* is a special prayer recited after death. It has such a shivering tone that even those who are not familiar with Muslim customs can tell that it is about the irreversible, the end. Tonight, *sela* is followed by loud announcements from minarets calling people to the streets in the name of God, to save the president, the democracy, the nation ... The tune of death now shares the sky with jets, the delirious '*Allahu akbar*'s of Erdoğan supporters and the soldiers' cries for help. And I remember the poem that started everything: 'The minarets are our bayonets/ The domes our helmets/The mosques our barracks/ And the faithful our soldiers.' It was Erdoğan who recited the poem at a public event in 1999, leading to him being imprisoned for four months for 'inciting religious hatred', and transforming him first into a martyr for democracy, then a ruthless leader. And after seventeen years, on the night of the coup the poem sounds like a self-fulfilling prophecy, a promise that has been kept at the cost of a country.

*   *   *

We have learned over time that coups in Turkey end the same way regardless of who initiated them. It's like the rueful quote from the former England footballer turned TV pundit Gary Lineker, that football is a simple game played for 120 minutes, and at the end the Germans win on penalties. In Turkey, coups are played out over forty-eight-hour curfews, and the leftists are locked up at the end. Then afterwards, of course, another generation of progressives is rooted out, leaving the country's soul even more barren than it was before.

As I watch the pro-government news channels throughout the night it becomes clearer by the minute that it is business as usual. Pictures and videos come through of arrested soldiers lying naked in the streets under the boots of civilians – as leftists lay under army boots after the coup in 1980 – and the news channels and the government trolls on social media, not at all paralysed like the rest of us, present us with the perspective they deem most appropriate: 'Thanks to Erdoğan's call, the people saved our democracy.'

'*Allahu akbar*'s multiply on my street, accompanied by machine-gun shots from the circulating cars. After so many years spent under AKP rule, devotion to the army has apparently been replaced by religious commitment to Erdoğan. We are watching his face and name become the emblems of the new Turkey we'll wake up to. Beneath the madness and the noise a carefully crafted propaganda machine is fully operational, already preparing the new political realm that will come into being in the morning. And having long been a critic of Erdoğan's regime, as dawn breaks it becomes *Kristall*-clear that there won't be a place for people like me in this new democracy.

Watching a disaster occur has a sedating effect; like millions of people around the country, I am numb. As our sense of helplessness grows along with the calamity, the cacophony transforms into a single siren, a constant refrain: 'There's no longer anything you can do; this is the end.' The global news channels jump in. For the rest of the world, the night's events are like the opening scene of a political thriller, but in fact this is the climax, the dénouement. It has been a very long and exhausting film, unbearably painful viewing for those of us who were forced to watch or take part. And I remember how it began: with a populist coming to town. Which is why, as the British and American TV anchors put hasty questions to the studio analysts, I feel like saying, 'As our story ends, yours is only just beginning.' A bleak dawn breaks.

I remember the exact day I experienced dawn for the first time. I woke up early one morning to the sound of the radio playing loudly in the living room, and found my mother and father chain smoking as they listened to a coup being declared. Their faces darkened as the day broke. It was 12 September 1980, and I looked up at the clear blue sky and said to myself, 'Oh, this must be what they call dawn.' I was eight, and one of the most vicious military coups in modern history was just getting started. My mother was silently crying, as she was to do frequently for several years after that dawn.

From that day forth, like millions of other children with parents who wanted a fair, equal and free Turkey, I grew up on the defeated side; among those who always had to be careful and who were, as my mother told me whenever I did less than perfectly at school, 'obliged to be smarter than those in power because we are up against them'. On the night of 15 July 2016 'we', as ever, were smarter than 'them', as we combined penetrating analysis with brilliant sarcasm. But in every square of every city in the country, raging crowds were playing the endgame, perhaps not as smartly, yet with devastating effect.

On 15 July 2016, my nephew Max Ali was the same age I was on 12 September 1980. He is one and a half years older than his brother, Can Luka. They are half-Turkish, half-American, and they live in the US. They were supposed to have gone home to America on 16 July, after a vacation spent with their *babaanne* – 'grandmother' in Turkish – my mother. Max Ali is a religious devotee of *babaanne* breakfasts. He is one of the lucky few on the planet who know of epic Turkish breakfasts, and he believes only *babaanne* knows how to make them. As a family, we're always proud that he chooses tomatoes and Turkish cheese over Cheerios, which my father calls 'animal food'. Had they not experienced the dawn during the coup their memories of *babaanne* would have been limited to indulgent breakfasts. But instead of heading to the airport that morning, as day broke they watched their *babaanne* crying and chain smoking in front of the TV. My mother told me Max Ali asked the same question I'd asked thirty-six years before: 'Did something bad happen to Turkey?' *Babaanne* was too tired to tell him that every generation in this country has its own dark memory of a dawn. She gave the same answer she had given me thirty-six years previously: 'It is complicated, my dear.'

How and why Turkish democracy was finally done away with by a ruthless populist and his growing band of supporters on the night of 15 July 2016 is a long and complicated story. The aim of this book is not to tell how we lost our democracy, but to attempt to draw lessons from the process, for the benefit of the rest of the world. Of course, every country has its own set of specific conditions, and some of them choose to believe that their mature democracy and strong state institutions will protect them from such 'complications'. However, the striking similarities between what Turkey went through and what the Western world began to experience a short while later are too many to dismiss. There is something resembling a pattern to the political insanity that we choose to name 'rising populism', and that we are all experiencing to some extent. And although many of them cannot yet articulate it, a growing number of people in the West sense that they too may end up experiencing similar dark dawns.

'Turks must be watching us and laughing their asses off tonight,' read an American tweet on the night of Donald Trump's election victory less than five months after the failed coup attempt. We weren't. Well, maybe one or two smirks might have appeared. Behind those smirks, though, lay exasperation at having to watch the same soul-destroying movie all over again, and this time on the giant screen of US politics. We wore the same pained expression after Britain's Brexit referendum, during the Dutch and German elections, and whenever a right-wing populist leader popped up somewhere in Europe sporting the movement's signature sardonic, bumptious grin.

On the night of the US presidential election, on the day of the Brexit referendum result, or when some local populist fired up a surprisingly large crowd with a speech that sounded like total nonsense, many asked the same question in their different languages: 'Is this my country? Are these my people?' People in Turkey, after asking these questions for almost two decades and witnessing the gradual political and moral collapse of their homeland, regressed to another dangerous doubt: 'Are human beings evil by nature?' That question represents the final defeat of the human mind, and it takes a long and excruciating time to understand that it's actually the wrong question. The aim of this book is to convince its readers to spare themselves the time and the torture by fast-forwarding the horror movie they have recently found themselves in, and showing them how to spot the recurring patterns of populism, so that maybe they can be better prepared for it than we were in Turkey.

It doesn't matter if Trump or Erdoğan is brought down tomorrow, or if Nigel Farage had never become a leader of public opinion. The millions of people fired up by their message will still be there, and will still be ready to act upon the orders of a similar figure. And unfortunately, as we experienced in Turkey in a very destructive way, even if you are determined to stay away from the world of politics, the minions will find you, even in your own personal space, armed with their own set of values and ready to hunt down anybody who doesn't resemble themselves. It is better to acknowledge – and sooner rather than later – that this is not merely something imposed on societies by their often absurd leaders, or limited to digital covert operations by the Kremlin; it also arises from the grassroots. The malady of our times won't be restricted to the corridors of power in Washington or Westminster. The

horrifying ethics that have risen to the upper echelons
of politics will trickle down and multiply, come to your
town and even penetrate your gated community. It's a
new *zeitgeist* in the making. This is a historic trend, and
it is turning *the banality of evil* into the evil of banality.
For though it appears in a different guise in every
country, it is time to recognise that what is occurring
affects us all.

'So, *what can we do for you?*'
    The woman in the audience brings her hands together
compassionately as she asks me the question; her raised
eyebrows are fixed in a delicate balance between pity
and genuine concern. It is September 2016, only two
months after the failed coup attempt, and I am at a
London event for my book *Turkey: The Insane and
the Melancholy*. Under the spotlight on the stage I
pause for a second to unpack the invisible baggage of
the question: the fact that she is seeing me as a needy
victim; her confidence in her own country's immunity
from the political malaise that ruined mine; but most of
all, even after the Brexit vote, her unshaken assumption
that Britain is still in a position to help anyone. Her
inability to acknowledge that we are all drowning
in the same political insanity provokes me. I finally
manage to calibrate this combination of thoughts into
a not-so-intimidating response: 'Well, now I feel like a
baby panda waiting to be adopted via a website.'

This is a moment in time when many still believe that Donald Trump cannot be elected, some genuinely hope that the Brexit referendum won't actually mean Britain leaving the European Union, and the majority of Europeans assume that the new leaders of hate are only a passing infatuation. So my bitter joke provokes not even a smile in the audience.

I have already crossed the Rubicon, so why not dig deeper? 'Believe it or not, whatever happened to Turkey is coming towards you. This political insanity is a global phenomenon. So actually, what can *I* do for you?'

What I decided I could do was to draw together the political and social similarities in different countries to trace a common pattern of rising right-wing populism. In order to do this I have used stories, which I believe are not only the most powerful transmitters of human experience, but also natural penicillin for diseases of the human soul. I identified seven steps the populist leader takes to transform himself from a ridiculous figure to a seriously terrifying autocrat, while corrupting his country's entire society to its bones. These steps are easy to follow for would-be dictators, and therefore equally easy to miss for those who would oppose them, unless we learn to read the warning signs. We cannot afford to lose time focusing on conditions unique to each of our countries; we need to recognise these steps when they are taken, define a common pattern, and find a way to break it – together. In order to do this, we'll need to combine the experience of those countries that have already been subjected to this insanity with that of Western countries whose stamina has not yet been exhausted. Collaboration is urgently required, and this necessitates a global conversation. This book humbly aims to initiate one.

ONE

Create a Movement

'We *have* to take the deer! We have to!'

So says four year old Leylosh, shouting to emphasise the fact that we simply *must* put the imaginary deer on the infinitely large back seat of our imaginary car, which is already filled by several other animals, including a dinosaur we luckily managed to rescue from freezing. We are driving from Lewisburg, a once-thriving small farming town, sixty miles north of Harrisburg, Pennsylvania, to her granny's house in Istanbul, to deliver the Lego duck that we built and then cooked on a miniature stove. Leylosh is squinting in the imaginary wind and providing a scary winter soundtrack for our arduous journey: 'Oouuuuvvoouuuv!' Now and then she checks with a quick side glance to make sure I'm fully engaged. Satisfied with my powers of imagination, she turns back to reassure our passengers: 'Don't be afraid. We'll be at Granny's soon. We don't have to go to school today.'

In a less exciting parallel universe, she will have to go to kindergarten in fifteen minutes, and in an hour's time I'll have to give a lecture at Bucknell University, a liberal arts college, on 'rising populism' and my novel *The Time of Mute Swans*, which partly deals with how Turkey became the perfect case study for the topic. Leylosh's mother Sezi, a long-time friend who teaches at Bucknell, talked me into this, because she believes that American academia needs to hear about the Turkish experience and to be warned about the later stages of the Trump administration. It is therefore now time to stop teaching Leylosh how to 'kiss like a fish' and return to my real-life role: floating like the angel with a bugle in Bruegel's *The Fall of the Rebel Angels* to alarm the wool-gathering masses. Sezi keeps checking her watch. But neither Leylosh nor I are keen to get out of the imaginary car, and in a way, her reasons are no less political than mine.

Sezi is a fortepianist and an expert on eighteenth- and nineteenth-century musical instruments. Leylosh probably thinks all mothers play Chopin on antique pianos to persuade their daughters to eat their breakfast. It's doubtless no more unusual to her that her father is an anthropologist who periodically visits indigenous tribes in the Amazon rainforest. Her school, a kindergarten

16

for children whose parents work at the university, a safe haven for children of cosmopolitan academics in a small American town, is full of kids like her; they speak at least two languages, travel regularly between continents, and are blissfully unaware that what's normal to them is far from ordinary.

'She used to love going to school,' says Sezi. But lately the mornings have begun resounding with cries of 'No, Mom! No!' As Leylosh holds on to the door of our imaginary car, refusing to leave for school, her mother explains that this new attitude, like many other inconveniences in the US, began after Trump came to power. Herein lie the political troubles of the four-year-old Leylosh.

The morning after the election, Leylosh arrived at school with her mother. The three teachers were waiting at the door, hands on their hips and brandishing new sardonic smiles. 'It was as if they were telling us to "suck it up"!' says Sezi. 'They're all Trump supporters who are taking care of the children of Bernie or Hillary voters. The tension has been gradually mounting ever since, and it now affects the children.' Sezi stops to find the right words: 'These people, they changed all of a sudden, it's as if they are now a different species.'

As the Argentinian proverb goes, 'A small town is a vast hell.' This is especially the case in today's world, because the phenomenon of rising populism has a lot to do with the provinces. Small towns are often where people first encounter this social and political current. However, they wouldn't describe it as diligently as the political analysts – and even if they did, their concerns would go largely unheard. The mobilising narrative of the new political direction feeds on provincial perceptions of life and the world, perceptions that are seen as too archaic to be understood by cosmopolitans. The small, unsettling changes in the provinces can seem inconsequential in big cities, where monitoring one's neighbours is a lost habit. It is therefore only long after right-wing populism has been felt by those in the provinces that it is diagnosed by the political analysts and big media.

Sezi gives me more examples of how people's general attitudes towards one another in her small town changed after Trump's victory, examples that might sound insignificant to big-city folk: ostentatiously smirking when the *liberal academics* enter local restaurants, or not removing 'Make America Great Again' signs from front gardens months after the election, and so on. As the examples multiply, it's as if she's trying to describe a strange smell: 'It's like it was already there, boiling away silently, and Trump's victory activated something, some dark motion was unleashed.'

Something has indeed been unleashed around the Western world. In several countries an invisible, odourless gas is travelling from the provinces to the big cities: a gas formed of grudges. *A scent of an ending* is drifting through the air. The word is spreading. *Real people* are moving from small towns towards the big cities to finally have the chance to be *the captains of their souls*. Nothing will stay unchanged, they say. A new *we* is emerging. A *we* that probably does not include you, the worried reader of this book. And I remember how that sudden exclusion once felt.

'No, we are different. We are not a party, we're a movement.'
   It is autumn 2002, and a brand-new party called the Justice and Development Party, AKP, with a ridiculous lightbulb for an emblem, is participating in a Turkish general election for the first time. Being a political columnist, I travel around the country, stopping off in remote cities and small towns, to take the nation's pulse before polling day. As I sit with representatives of other, conventional parties in a coffee shop in a small town in central Anatolia, three men stand outside the circle, their eyebrows raised with an air of lofty impatience, waiting for me to finish my interview. I invite them to join us at the table, but they politely refuse, as if I am sitting in the middle of an invisible swamp they don't want to dirty themselves in. When the others eventually prepare to leave, they approach me as elegantly as macho Anatolians can. 'You may call us a movement, the movement of the virtuous,' the man says. 'We are more than a party. We will change everything in this

corrupt system.' He is ostentatiously proud, and rarely grants me eye contact.

The other two men nod approvingly as their extremely composed spokesman fires off phrases like 'dysfunctional system', 'new representatives of the people, not tainted by politics', 'a new Turkey with dignity'. Their unshakeable confidence, stemming from vague yet strongly held convictions, reminds me of the young revolutionary leftists I've written about for a number of years in several countries. They give off powerful, mystic vibes, stirring the atmosphere in the coffee shop of this desperate small town. They are like visiting disciples from a higher moral plane, their chins raised like young Red Guards in Maoist propaganda posters. When the other small-town politicians mock their insistence on the distinction between their 'movement' and other parties, the three men appear to gain in stature from the condescending remarks, like members of a religious cult who embrace humiliation to tighten the bonds of their inner circle.

Their spokesman taps his fist gently, but sternly, on the table to finish his speech: 'We are the people of Turkey. And when I say people, I mean *real people*.'

This is the first time I hear the term 'real people' used in this sense. The other politicians, from both left and right, are annoyed by the phrase, and protest mockingly: 'What's that supposed to mean? We're the real people of Turkey too.' But it's too late; the three men delight in being the original owners of the claim. It is theirs now.

After seeing the same scene repeat itself with little variation in several other towns, I write in my column: 'They will win.' I am teased by my colleagues, but in November 2002 the silly lightbulb party of the three men in the coffee shop becomes the new government of Turkey. The movement that gathered power in small towns all over the country has now ruled Turkey uninterrupted for seventeen years, changing everything, just as they promised.

'We have the same thing here. Exactly the same thing! But who are these real people?'

It's now May 2017, and I am first in London, then Warsaw, talking about *Turkey: The Insane and the Melancholy*, telling different audiences the story of how *real people* took over my country politically and socially, strangling all the others who they deemed *unreal*. People nod with concern, and every question-and-answer session starts with the same question: 'Where the hell did these *real people* come from?'

They recognise the lexicon, because the politicised and mobilised provincial grudge has announced its grand entrance onto the global stage with essentially the same statement in several countries: 'This is a movement, a new movement of real people beyond and above all political factions.' And now many want to know who these *real people* are, and why this *movement* has invaded the high table of politics. They speak of it as of a natural disaster, predictable only after it unexpectedly takes place. I am reminded of those who, each summer, are surprised by the heatwave in Scandinavia, and only then recall the climate-change news they read the previous winter. I tell them this 'new' phenomenon has been with us, boiling away, for quite some time.

In July 2017, a massive iceberg broke off from Antarctica. For several days the news channels showed the snow-white monster floating idly along. It was the majestic flagship of our age, whispering from screens around the world in creaking ice language: 'This is the final phase of the age of disintegration. *Everything that stands firm* will break off, everything will fall to pieces.' It wasn't a *spectre* but a solid monster telling the story of our times: that from the largest to the smallest entity on planet earth, nothing will remain as we knew it. The United Nations, that huge, impotent body created to foster global peace, is crumbling, while the smallest unit, the soul, is decomposing as it has never been before. A single second can be divided up into centuries during which the wealthy few prepare uncontaminated living spaces in which to live longer while tens of thousands of children in Yemen die of cholera, a pre-twentieth-century disease. The iceberg was silently screaming, *The centre cannot hold.*

The progressive movements that sprang up all around the world, from the World Trade Organization protests in Seattle in 1999 to the 2011 uprising in Cairo's Tahrir Square, were in many respects a response to these *fractured* times. In a world where more people are talking, but fewer are being heard, they wanted to tell the rest of humanity, through their bodies, that regardless of our differences we can, and indeed must, come together to find collective answers to our age of disintegration, otherwise everything will fall apart. They demanded justice and dignity. They demanded that the world realise that a counter-movement is necessary to reverse the global course of events. They showed us that retreat is not the only response to the global loss of hope. They were the ones who resisted the temptation to 'yield to the process of mere disintegration', and rejected the notion that it is 'a historical necessity'.* Their answer to disintegration was to create new, invigorating, temporary and miniature models of loose collectives in squares around the world. In several different languages they responded to the famous words of W.B. Yeats with the message that, if people unite, the centre *can* hold.

As time passed, however, many of these progressive movements ended up suppressed, marginalised or swallowed back into the conventional political system. For

---

* Karl Jaspers, Preface to Hannah Arendt, *The Origins of Totalitarianism* (Schocken, 1951).

several understandable reasons they couldn't accomplish what they started – not yet. However, their voice was clearly heard when they announced globally that representative democracy (abused by financial institutions and stripped of social justice) was undergoing its biggest crisis since the Second World War.

Today we are witnessing the response to similar fears of an entirely different mass of people, one with a more limited vocabulary, smaller dreams for the world, and less faith in the collective survival of humanity. They too say that they want to change the status quo, but they want to do it to build a world in which they are among the lucky few who survive under the leadership of a strong man. It is no coincidence that 'wall', whether literal or virtual, has become the watchword among rising right-wing political movements. 'Yes, the world is disintegrating,' they say, 'and we, the *real people*, want to make sure we're on the sunny side of the dividing wall.' It is not that they want to stand by and watch babies die in the Mediterranean, it is just that *they* don't want to die as well. What we are hearing, as it carries from the provinces to the big cities, is the survival cry of those whose fear of drowning in the rising sea of disintegration trumps their interest in the survival of others. And so, ruthlessly, they *move*.

*　　*　　*

Political movements are promises of transition from actuality to potentiality – unlike political parties, which must operate as part of actuality, playing the game but standing still. This is why, from Turkey to the United States, including the most developed countries with their seemingly strong democratic institutions, such as France, the UK and Germany, we have seen people assemble behind relentless, audacious populist leaders, in order to move together and attack the actuality they call *the establishment*; to attack the game itself, deeming it dysfunctional and corrupt. *A movement of real people* is the new *zeitgeist*, a promise to bring back human dignity by *draining the swamp* of the stagnant water that politics has become. In other words, *les invisibles*, the masses, long considered to be indifferent to politics and world affairs, are globally withdrawing their assumed consent from the current representative system, and the sound of it is like a chunk of ice breaking off from Antarctica.

The job of changing the global course of events is, of course, too big a task for the fragile *I*, and so *we* is making a comeback in the world of politics and ethics. And this comeback is at the heart of the global phenomenon that we are witnessing. *We* wants to depart from the mainland of political language, dismantle it and build a new language for the *real people*. If one wants to know who the *real people* are, one must ask the question, what is *we*? Or why is it that *I* don't want to be *I* any more, but *we*?

* * *

25

It is one of those crowded Sundays on the European side of the Bosporus in the summer of 2015. Sunday is the day that the upper-middle classes of Istanbul move *en masse* to the cafés on the seaside for the famous Turkish breakfast, which lasts more or less the entire day. The cafés are located alongside the Ottoman fortress walls, where bloody wars were fought to enable us to one day have these glorious feasts and to be irritated when our order is late. There is a family over there, on the pavement, in their best outfits. Not wealthy enough to sit at the cafés, but able to make ends meet so that they can stroll through the richest neighbourhood on the Bosporus and watch the arduous weekend breakfast campaign. The two small kids are being led by their young mother, who is trying hard not to make it too obvious that this is their first time in this part of the city. The father seems to be searching for something on the ground as he walks. Then he stops, and points to a spot on the pavement. 'Here! Here!' he shouts happily. 'This is the one. This one. I put that there.' His gaze then proudly travels the full length of the paving. 'This is the longest road in Istanbul,' he says, 'and *we* made it.'

I have always wondered whether the families of the fallen workers of the great bridges, great tunnels, great roads, ever visit the little memorial plaques attached to those constructions. Do they take pictures in front of them, pointing at a name? And is it essential that

26

they describe the road as 'the longest', the tunnel 'the deepest', their country 'the greatest'? Otherwise, will their relative's life and death be meaningless? Some of us cannot and never will understand why a man who can hardly make a living is proud of the fact that Erdoğan's is 'the greatest palace', or why he rejoices when he hears that the daily cost of running that palace is ten times more than he earns in a year. For many of those who are privileged enough to be in a position to try to analyse the important matters of big politics, the ordinary man's feeling of smallness and the rage it engenders are inaccessible, and so it is equally hard for them to comprehend how that smallness might desperately crave to be part of a *we* that promises greatness.

'I play to people's fantasies. People want to believe that something is the biggest and the greatest and the most spectacular. I call it truthful hyperbole. It is an innocent form of exaggeration – and a very effective form of promotion.'

In his debut work of literature, *The Art of the Deal*,* Donald Trump was already describing the 'truthful hyperbole' that would later put him in the White House. He must be proud to have demonstrated that in order to become the American president he had no

---

* Donald J. Trump with Tony Schwartz, *The Art of the Deal* (Random House, 1987).

need to read any books other than his own. Trump knew one simple fact about people that many of us choose to ignore: that even though individualism as a concept has been elevated for many decades, the ordinary man still needs a shepherd to lead him to greatness. He knew how diminishing and disappointing it can feel to realise that you are only mediocre, in a world where you have constantly been told that you can be anything you want to be.

He also knew that the call to break the imaginary chains of slavery preventing the *real people* from reaching greatness would resonate with his supporters, regardless of the fact that it sounded absurd to those who *had* had the chance to become what they wanted to be. 'It's not you,' he told them. 'It's *them* who prevent us from being great.' He gave them something solid to hate, and they gave him their votes. And once he started speaking in the name of *we* – as has happened many times over the course of history – they were ready to sacrifice themselves. As Americans know very well from their own constitution, the words 'We, the people' can build a new country and bring empires to their knees. And believe it or not, even the British, a people who take pride in not being easily moved, are also not immune to the allure of *we*.

* * *

'We have fought against the multinationals, we have fought against the big merchant banks, we have fought against big politics, we have fought against lies, corruption and deceit ... [This is] a victory for real people, a victory for ordinary people, a victory for decent people.'

Although this may sound like Salvador Allende, Chile's Marxist leader, speaking after his election victory in 1970, it was in fact Nigel Farage, the erstwhile leader of UKIP – and incidentally a former banker himself. He uttered these words on the morning of 24 June 2016, the day after Britain's Brexit referendum. He too was using the age-old magic of speaking in the name of 'the people'. On the same day, however, many cosmopolitan Londoners, who were automatically excluded from this inflaming narrative, found themselves wondering who these *real people* were, and why they bore such a grudge against the big cities and the educated. And those who were old enough were beginning to hear echoes sounding from across the decades.

After the horrific experiences of the Second World War, not many people in Western Europe expected the masses ever again to lust after becoming a single totality. Most happily believed that if humans were free to choose what they could buy, love and believe, they would be content. For more than half a century, the word *I* was promoted in the public sphere by the ever-grinning market economy and its supporting characters, the dominant political discourse and mainstream culture. But now *we* has returned as the very essence of *the movement*, burnishing it with a revolutionary glow, and many have found themselves unprepared for this sudden resurrection.

Their voice has been so loud and so unexpected that worried critics have struggled to come up with an up-to-date political lexicon with which to describe it, or counter it. The critical mainstream intelligentsia scrambled to gather ammunition from history, but unfortunately most of it dated back to the Nazi era. The word 'fascism' sounded passé, childish even, and 'authoritarianism' or 'totalitarianism' were too 'khaki' for this Technicolor beast in a neoliberal world. Yet during the last couple of years numerous political self-help books filled with quotes from George Orwell have been hastily written, and all of a sudden Hannah Arendt's *The Origins of Totalitarianism* is back on the bestseller lists after a sixty-eight-year hiatus. The hip-sounding term that the mainstream intelligentsia chose to use for this retro lust for totality was 'rising populism'.

'Rising populism' is quite a convenient term for our times. It both conceals the right-wing ideological content of the movements in question, and ignores the troubling question of the shady desire of *I* to melt into *we*. It masterfully portrays the twisted charismatic leaders who are mobilising the masses as mad men, and diligently dismisses the masses as deceived, ignorant people. It also washes away the backstory that might reveal how we ended up in this mess. In addition to this, there is the problem that the populists do not define themselves as 'populists'. In a supposedly post-ideology world, they are free to claim to be beyond politics, and above political institutions.

Political thought has not been ready to fight this new fight either. One of the main stumbling blocks is that the critics of the phenomenon have realised that 'rising populism' is the strange fruit of the current practice of democracy. As they looked deeper into the question they soon discovered that it wasn't a wound that, all of a sudden, appeared on the body politic, but was in fact a mutant child of crippled representative democracy.

Moreover, a new ontological problem was at play thanks to the right-wing spin doctors. Academics, journalists and the well-educated found themselves included in the *enemy of the people* camp, part of the corrupt establishment, and their criticism of, or even their carefully constructed comments on, this political phenomenon were considered to be oppressive by the *real people* and the movement's spin doctors. It was difficult for them to adapt to the new environment in which they had become the 'oppressive elite' – if not 'fascists' – despite the fact that some of them had dedicated their lives to the emancipation of the very masses who now held them in such contempt. One of them was my grandmother.

*   *   *

How to Lose a Country

'Are they now calling me a fascist, Ece?'

My grandmother, one of the first generation of teachers in the young Turkish republic, a committed secular woman who had spent many years bringing literacy to rural children, turned to me one evening in 2005 while we were watching a TV debate featuring AKP spin doctors and asked, 'They did say "fascist", right?' She dismissed my attempt to explain the peculiarities of the new political narratives and exclaimed, 'What does that even mean, anyway? *Oppressive elite*! I am not an elite. I starved and suffered when I was teaching village kids in the 1950s.'

Her arms, having been folded defensively, were now in the air, her finger pointing as she announced, as if addressing a classroom, 'No! Tomorrow I am going to go down to their local party centre and tell them that I am as real as them.' And she did, only to return home speechless, dragging her exhausted eighty-year-old legs off to bed at midday for an unprecedented nap of defeat. The only words I could get out of her were: 'They are different, Ece. They are ...' Despite her excellent linguistic skills, she couldn't find an appropriate adjective.

I was reminded of my grandmother's endeavour when a seventy-something American woman approached me with some hesitation after a talk I gave at Harvard University in 2017. Evidently one of those people who are hesitant about bothering others with personal matters, she gave me a fast-forward version

32

of her own story: she had been a Peace Corps volunteer in the 1960s, teaching English to kids in a remote Turkish town, then a dedicated high school teacher in the USA, and since her retirement she had become a serious devotee of Harvard seminars. She was no less stunned than my grandmother at the fact that Trump voters were calling her a member of the 'oppressive elite'. She said, 'I try to explain myself to them when we talk about politics, but ...' A ruthless political narrative that labelled her lifelong labours as both unimportant and oppressive was gaining traction. In this new political scenario, she found herself trying to crawl out of the deep hole that had been dug for elites, a hole that was proving too deep for her frail legs. The more serious problem was that the *real people* never asked her to join them, or offered to help her climb out of the hole. All they demanded from her was 'respect'.

'Respect is something I hear a lot about from Trump voters. The spirit of the sentiment is often: "Maybe Trump's a jerk, maybe he won't do what he says he will, but he acts as if people like me are important, and the people who disrespect me aren't."'

In September 2016 the *Chicago Tribune* published a Bloomberg opinion piece by Megan McArdle.* As she

---

* Megan McArdle, '"Deplorables" and the Myth of the Single-Issue Voter', *Bloomberg*, 19 September 2016.

had expressed before in other columns, McArdle was stunned by the fact that any conversation with Trump supporters was usually brought to a halt by the word 'respect'. When Trump entered the scene, bucketloads of 'respect' flushed through American politics, and Hillary Clinton's 'deplorables' comment about Trump supporters gave them yet another angle to exploit. Suddenly the media was questioning its own ability to respect ordinary people. Self-criticism among journalists, together with the massive attacks on the media from Trump supporters for being disrespectful towards *real people*, became impossible to ignore. So much so that after the election the *New York Times* opened a 'Trump voters only' section in which they could express themselves free from the condescending filter of the elitist media. Even if the new platform might have functioned as a rich source of raw research material for academics, it was definitely a triumph for Trump voters in their quest for gaining respect, a victorious battle in the long war of recognition.

We always holds its challengers to ethical standards (such as objectivity) that it does not itself feel obliged to meet, because the original owners of *we* have a monopoly on morality and the privilege of being the *real* voice of the masses. End of story. Critical voices become so paralysed that they don't notice that the 'respect' *we* demand of them is actually an unquestioning silence.

The magic word 'respect' is also frequently used by the right-wing Hungarian leader Viktor Orbán. 'Respect to the Hungarians!' was his party's 2014 European Parliament electoral slogan. Between then and the end of 2017, Orbán relentlessly reiterated the central importance of respect. He demanded respect from Germany, the United States and the EU, and when attacked for his xenophobic policies he replied: 'According to my thinking, this is a sign of respect.' He announced his solidarity with Poland because Poland wasn't respected enough, and offered his respect to Trump, Vladimir Putin and Erdoğan. He also complained that 'respect is a scarce commodity in Europe', and asserted that only respect could save the continent.

Erdoğan likewise introduced excessive amounts of 'respect' into Turkish politics after he came to power in 2002. He repeatedly demonstrated to the Turkish people that respect no longer had to be earned, it could simply be unconditionally demanded. Whenever there were serious poll-rigging claims, he demanded respect for 'my people and their choices', just as he demanded respect for court decisions only when they resulted in his opponents being imprisoned. However, when the Constitutional Court decided to release journalists arrested for criticising him, he said, 'I don't respect the court decision and I won't abide by it.' As with Orbán, Trump and others, respect is a one-way street for Erdoğan: he only accepts being on the receiving end.

* * *

'[Respect] is what Putin really wants,' wrote Fiona Hill in a piece for the Brookings Institution's website in February 2015.* She continued, 'He wants respect in the old-fashioned, hard-power sense of the word.'

'You come to me and say, "Give me justice." But you don't ask with respect.' This quote comes not from another respect-obsessed political leader, but from Don Corleone, in the opening scene of *The Godfather*. One might easily mix them up, because the global circuit of exchanged respect (Geert Wilders respecting Farage, Farage respecting Trump, Trump respecting Putin, Putin asking for more respect for Trump, and all the way back round again, much as Hitler and Stalin once voiced their respect for one another) has started to sound like some supranational mafia conversation. The web of respect among authoritarian leaders has expanded so much that one might forget that this whole masquerade started on a smaller scale, with a seemingly harmless question. It started when the ordinary people began transforming themselves into *real people* by demanding a little bit of political politeness: 'Don't we deserve some simple respect?'

*　*　*

---

* Fiona Hill, 'This is What Putin Really Wants', *Brookings*, 24 February 2015.

But here's how the chain of events goes further down the line when respect becomes a political commodity. When the *real people* become a political movement, their initial, rhetorical question is this: 'Do our beliefs, our way of life, our choices not matter at all?' Of course, nobody can possibly say that they do not, and so the leaders of the movement begin to appear in public, and take to the stage as respected, equal contributors to the political discussion.

The next password is *tolerance*, tolerance for differences. Then some opinion leaders, who've noticed social tensions arising from polarisation in the public sphere, throw in the term *social peace*. It sounds wise and soothing, so nobody wants to dismiss it. However, as the movement gains momentum, tolerance and respect become the possessions of its members, which only they can grant to others, and the leader starts pushing the 'social peace' truce to the limits, demanding tolerance and respect every time he or she picks a new fight.

But at a particular point in time, respect becomes a scarce commodity. For Turkey, this invisible shift happened in 2007, on the election night that brought the AKP a second term in power. Erdoğan said, 'Those who did not vote for us are also different colours of Turkey.' At the time, for many political journalists the phrase sounded like the embracing voice of a compassionate father seeking social peace. However, not long afterwards, Erdoğan started speaking Godfather. He stopped asking for respect and raised the bar, warning almost everyone, from European politicians to small-town public figures, that they were required to 'know their place'. And when that warning was not enough, he followed it up with threats. On 11 March 2017, Turkey was mired in a diplomatic row with Germany and the Netherlands after they banned Turkish officials from campaigning in their countries in support of a referendum on boosting the Turkish president's powers. Erdoğan said, 'If Europe continues this way, no European in any part of the world can walk safely on the streets.' In threatening an entire continent, he'd become the cruel Michael Corleone of *The Godfather Part II*.

Even for those countries that have only recently begun to experience a similar social and political process, this chain of events is already beginning to seem like a cliché. Nevertheless, the way in which the logic of contemporary identity politics serves this process is still relatively novel, and is rarely discussed. In the twenty-first century it's much easier for right-wing populist movements to demand respect by wrapping themselves in the bulletproof political membrane of a cultural and political identity and exploiting a political correctness that has disarmed critical commentators. Moreover, the use of a sacrosanct identity narrative turns the tables, shining the interrogator's lamp on the critics of the movement instead of on the movement itself, making them ask, 'Are we not respectful enough, and is that why they're so enraged?' As the opposition becomes mired in compromise, the movement begins to ask the probing questions: 'Are you sure you're not intimidating us out of arrogance? Can you be certain this is not discrimination?'

And we all know what happens when self-doubting intellect encounters ruthless, self-evident ignorance; to believers in the self-evident, the basic need to question sounds like not having an answer, and embarrassed silence in the face of brazen shamelessness comes across as speechless awe. Politicised ignorance then proudly pulls up a chair alongside members of the entire political spectrum and dedicates itself to dominating the table, elbowing everyone continually while demanding, 'Are you sure your arm was in the right place?' And the opposition finds itself having to bend out of shape to follow the new rules of the table in order to be able to keep sitting there.

'We become increasingly uncomfortable when people take advantage of our freedom and ruin things here.'
These words came from a Dutch politician, but not the notorious xenophobe Geert Wilders. They are from his opponent, the Dutch prime minister and leader of the centre-right Liberal Party, Mark Rutte, in a letter to 'all Dutch people' published on 23 January 2017.

Although the words seemingly referred to anyone who 'took advantage', they were in fact aimed at immigrants. Rutte's opposition to right-wing populism was being distorted by the fact that he felt obliged to demonstrate that he shared the concerns of the *real people*: ordinary, decent people. He must have felt that in order to keep sitting at the top table of politics, he had to compromise. And this is the man who two months later would bring joy to Dutch liberals by beating Wilders. Many Dutch voters accepted, albeit unwillingly, the new reality in which the least worst option is the only choice. The manufactured *we* is now strong enough not only to mobilise and energise supporters of the movement by giving them a long-forgotten taste of being part of a larger entity, but to affect the rest of the political sphere by pushing and pulling the opposition until it transforms itself irreversibly. It creates a new normality, which takes us all closer towards insanity.

'*We are Muslims too.*'

This was the most frequent introduction offered by social democrat participants in TV debates in the first years that the AKP held power in Turkey. Just as what constituted being part of the *we*, 'the real, ordinary, decent people', meant supporting Brexit in Britain or accepting a bit of racism in the Netherlands, so did being conservative, provincial Sunni Muslim in Turkey.

Once the parameters had been set by the original owners of *we*, everyone else started trying to prove that they too prayed – just in private. Soon, Arabic words most people had never heard in their lives before became part of the public debate, and social democrats tried to compete with the 'real Muslims' despite their limited knowledge of religion. The AKP spin doctors were quick to put new religious concepts into circulation, and critics were forever on the back foot, constantly having to prepare for pop quizzes on ancient scriptures.

One might wonder what would happen if you passed all the tests for being as real as them, as I did once. In 2013, after studying the Quran for over a year while writing my novel *Women Who Blow on Knots*, I was ready for the quiz. When the book was published I was invited to take part in a TV debate with a veiled AKP spin doctor – a classic screen charade that craves a political catfight between a secular and a religious woman. As I recited the verse in Arabic that gave the title to my novel and answered her questions on the Quran she smiled patronisingly and said, 'Well done!' I was politely reminded of the fact that I was at best an apprentice of the craft she had mastered, and somehow owned. She made it very clear that people like me could only ever inhabit the outer circle of the *real people*. No matter how hard we toiled, we could only ever be members of the despised elite. Any attempt to hang out at one of Nigel Farage's 'real people's pubs' or a Trump supporters' barbecue would doubtless end with a similar patronising smile, and maybe a condescending pat on the shoulder: 'Way to go, kiddo!'

One of the interesting and rarely mentioned aspects of this process is that at times the cynical and disappointed citizens, even though they are critical of *the movement*, secretly enjoy the fact that the table has been messed up. The shocked face of the establishment amuses them. They know that the massive discontent of the neglected masses will eventually produce an equally massive political reaction, and they tend to believe that *the movement* might have the potential to be this long-expected corrective response to injustice. Until they find out it is not. 'The insinuation that the exterminator is not wholly in the wrong,' says J.P. Stern, 'is the secret belief of the age of Kafka and Hitler.'* The limitless confidence of *the movement* is not, therefore, entirely based on its own merit; the undecided, as well as many an adversary, can furnish the movement with confidence through their own hesitations. After all, there's nothing wrong with saying the establishment is corrupt, right? By keeping its ideological goals vague and its words sweet, the movement seduces many by allowing them to attribute their own varying ideals or disappointments to it. What is wrong with being *decent*

---

* Quoted in Michael Wood, *Literature and the Taste of Knowledge* (Cambridge University Press, 2009).

and *real* anyway? The vagueness of the narrative and the all-embracing *we* allow the movement's leader to create contradictory, previously impossible alliances to both the right and the left of the political spectrum. The leader, thanks to the ideological shapelessness of the movement, can also attract finance from opposite ends of the social strata, drawing from the poorest to the richest. Most importantly, as the leader speaks of exploitation, inequality, injustice and consciousness, borrowing terminology and references from both right- and left-wing politics, growing numbers of desperate, self-doubting people, and a fair few prominent opinion-makers besides, find themselves saying: 'He actually speaks a lot of sense. Nobody can say that a large part of society wasn't neglected and dismissed, right?'

'I don't understand how they won. I'm telling you, lady, not a single passenger said they were voting for them. So who did *vote for these guys?'*

This was the standard chat of taxi drivers in Turkey after the AKP's second election victory. As a consequence, 'So who *did* vote for these guys?' became a popular intro to many a newspaper column. Clearly neither taxi drivers nor the majority of opinion-piece writers could make sense of the unceasing success of the movement, despite rising concerns about it. After hearing the same question several times, I eventually answered one of the taxi drivers with a line that became the intro to one of my own columns: 'Evidently they all catch the bus.'

After the Brexit referendum, many people in London doubtless asked themselves a similar question. If I'd been a British columnist, the title for my column might have been 'The Angry Cod Beats European Ideals'. Among the groups who voted Leave in the referendum were Scottish fishermen, who have obsessed for many years over the fact that European fishermen were allowed to fish in Scottish waters, as well as pissed off about an array of other European things that are of next to no consequence to Scotland. Similarly, in countries such as Hungary and Poland where right-wing populism is in control of the political discourse there has always been a 'condescending Brussels elite', or 'the damn Germans', who stand in the way of better lives for ordinary men, as well as the nation's 'greatness'.

I am aware that what I have written above might seem like the condescending remarks of a *cosmopolitan, unreal person*, and that there is, of course, a real and solid sense of victimhood behind all of these new movements: many of their members are indeed the people who catch the bus, and who have seen the price of their fish and chips rise. It would therefore, as Greek economist and former finance minister Yanis Varoufakis says, be inconsequential mental gymnastics for intellectuals to analyse these movements only 'psychoanalytically, culturally, anthropologically, aesthetically, and of course in terms of identity politics'.* And I agree with him on the fact that 'the unceasing class war that has been waged against the poor since the late 1970s' has been intentionally omitted from the narrative, and carefully kept outside the mainstream global discussion. Moreover, these right-wing populist movements can, in fact, also be seen as newly-built, fast-moving vehicles for the rich, a means for the ruling class to get rid of the regulations that restrain the free-market economy by throwing the entire field of politics into disarray. After all, there is certainly real suffering, genuine victimhood behind these movements.

However, they do not *only* emerge from real suffering, but also from manufactured victimhood. In fact, it is the latter that provides the movement with most of its energy and creates its unique characteristics.

In Turkey, the manufactured victimhood was that religious people were oppressed and humiliated by the secular elite of the establishment. For Brexiteers it is that they have been deprived of Britain's greatness. For Trump voters it is that Mexicans are stealing their jobs. For Polish right-wing populists it is Nazis committing crimes against humanity on their soil without their participation and the global dismissal of the nation's fierce resistance to the German invasion in 1939.

---

* Yanis Varoufakis, 'The High Cost of Denying Class War', *Project Syndicate*, 8 December 2017.

For Germany's AfD (Alternative für Deutschland) it is the 'lazy Greeks' who benefit from hard-working *real* Europeans, etc. The content really doesn't matter, because in the later stages it changes constantly, transforms and is replaced in relation to emerging needs and the aims of the movement.

And every time the masses adapt to the new narrative, regardless of the fact that it often contradicts how the movement began in the first place. In Turkey, the Gülen movement, a supranational religious network led by an imam who currently lives in Pennsylvania, was an integral part of Erdoğan's movement, until it was labelled terrorist overnight. The same AKP ministers and party members who had knelt to kiss the imam Fethullah Gülen's hand were, less than twenty-four hours later, falling over themselves to curse him, and none of Erdoğan's supporters questioned this shift. Doubtless Trump voters did not find it odd when the FBI, Trump's very best friend during the probing of Hillary Clinton's emails scandal, all of a sudden became 'disgraceful' after it started questioning whether Trump's election campaign had colluded with the Russian government. Instead, Fox News called the FBI a 'criminal cabal' and started talking about a possible coup, confident that Trump's supporters would follow the new lead, feeling, as their leader did, victimised by the disrespectful establishment. Once the identification of the masses and the movement with the leader begins, the ever-changing nature of the content of the manufactured victimhood becomes insignificant. And when the leader is a master of 'truthful hyperbole', the content even becomes irrelevant.

But how, one might ask, did the masses, dismissing the entirety of world history, start moving against their own interests, and against what are so obviously the wrong targets? Not the cheap-labour-chasing giant corporations, but poor Mexicans; not the cruelty of free-market economics, but French fishermen; not the causes of poverty, but the media. How did they become so vindictive towards such irrelevant groups? Why do they demand respect from the educated elite, but not from the owners of multinational companies? And why did they do this by believing in a man just because he was seemingly 'one of them'? 'This is almost childish,' one might think. 'It seems infantile.' And it is. That's why, first and foremost, such leaders need to infantilise the people.

Infantilisation of the masses through infantilisation of the political language is crucial, as we shall see in the next chapter. Otherwise you cannot make them believe that they can all climb into an imaginary car and travel across continents together. Besides, once you infantilise the common political narrative, it becomes easier to mobilise the masses, and from then on you can promise them anything.

Sezi promises Leylosh an 'evening surprise' to persuade her to go to school. I ask what the surprise is. 'There is no surprise, but she won't remember probably,' Sezi says, before laughing devilishly. 'And if she does, I'll just make something up.'

TWO

Disrupt Rationale/
Terrorise Language

'... and that was when Chávez gathered his loyal friends
under a fig tree on top of a hill. They all swore on the
Bible. That's how and why the revolution started.'
The Venezuelan ambassador to Turkey accompanied his closing words with a rehearsed hand gesture,
indicating Heaven above, from whence the irrefutable
truth had come. His finger lingered there for a dramatic
moment, pointing at the ceiling of the Ankara Faculty
of Law. His presentation was over, and as his fellow
panellist it was my turn to address the question of how
the Venezuelans managed to make a revolution.

This was 2007, a year after I'd published *We are
Making a Revolution Here, Señorita!*, a series of interviews I'd conducted in the *barrios* of Caracas about
how the grassroots movement had started to organise

itself in communes long before Hugo Chávez became president. I was therefore quite certain that the real story did not involve mythical components like fig trees on hilltops and messages direct from Heaven. I had maintained a bewildered smile in silence for as long as I could, expecting His Excellency sitting next to me to apply a little common sense, but I found my mouth slowly becoming a miserable prune, as my face adopted the expression of a rational human being confronted by a true believer. It was already too late to dismiss his fairy tale as nonsense, so I simply said, 'Well, it didn't really happen like that.' There were a few long seconds of tense silence as our eyes locked, mine wide open, his glassy, and my tone changed from sarcasm to genuine curiosity: 'You know that, right?' His face remained blank, and I realised, with a feeling somewhere between compassion and fear, that this well-educated diplomat was obliged to tell this fairy tale.

Hugo Chávez's name was already in the hall of fame of 'The Great Populists'. He was criminalising every critical voice as coming from an *enemy of the real people* while claiming to be not only the sole representative of the entire nation, but the nation itself. Evidently he was also concocting self-serving tales and making them into official history, infantilising a nation and rendering basic human intelligence a crime against the *proceso*, the overall transformation of the country to so-called socialism – or a version of it, tailored by Chávez himself.

The ambassador looked like a tired child who just wanted to get to the end of the story and go to sleep. I didn't know then that in a short while grappling with fairy tales would become our daily business in Turkey, and that we would be obliged to prove that what everybody had seen with their own eyes had really happened.

'It is alleged that the American continent was discovered by Columbus in 1492. In fact, Muslim scholars reached the American continent 314 years before Columbus, in 1178. In his memoirs, Christopher Columbus mentions the existence of a mosque on top of a hill on the coast of Cuba.'

On 15 November 2014, President Erdoğan told this tale to a gathering of Latin American Muslim leaders. The next day journalists around the world reported on the Turkish president's bombastic contribution to history, hiding their smirks behind polite sentences that confidently implied, 'Of course it didn't happen like that, but you know that anyway.'

Neither Brexit nor Trump had happened yet. The Western journalists therefore didn't know that their smirks would become prunes when rationality proved helpless against not only the nonsense of a single man, but the mesmerised eyes of millions who believed his nonsense. Had they been asked, Venezuelans or Turks could have told those journalists all about the road of despair that leads from a mosque on a Cuban hilltop to a hilltop in Ankara where nonsense becomes official history, and an entire nation succumbs to exhaustion. They could also have explained how the populist engine, intent on infantilising political language and destroying reason, begins its work by saying, 'We know very well who Socrates is! You can't deceive us about that evil guy any more!' And you say, 'Hold on. Who said anything about Socrates?!'

'With populism on the rise all over Europe, we every so often face the challenge of standing up to populist positions in public discourse. In this workshop, participants learn to successfully stand their ground against populist arguments. By means of hands-on exercises and tangible techniques, participants learn to better assess populist arguments, to quickly identify their strengths and weaknesses, to concisely formulate their own arguments, and to confidently and constructively confront people with populist standpoints.'

I am quoting from an advertisement for the Institut für Argumentationskompetenz, a German think-tank. The title of the course they offer clients is 'How to Use Logic Against Populists'. Evidently the helplessness of rationality and language against the warped logic of populism has already created considerable demand in the politics market, and as a consequence martial-arts techniques for defensive reasoning are now being taught. The course involves two days of workshops, and attendees are invited to bring their own, no doubt maddening, personal experiences along. Were I to attend the course with my sixteen years' worth of Turkish experiences, I would humbly propose, at the risk of having Aristotle turn in his grave, opening this beginner's guide to populist argumentation by presenting Aristotle's famous syllogism 'All humans are mortal. Socrates is a human. Therefore Socrates is mortal':

ARISTOTLE: All humans are mortal.

POPULIST: That is a totalitarian statement.

ARISTOTLE: Do you not think that all humans are mortal?

POPULIST: Are you interrogating me? Just because we are not *citizens* like you, but *people*, we are ignorant, is that it? Maybe we are, but we know about real life.

ARISTOTLE: That is irrelevant.

POPULIST: Of course it's irrelevant to you. For years you and your kind have ruled this place, saying the people are irrelevant.

ARISTOTLE: Please, answer my question.

POPULIST: The real people of this country think otherwise. Our response is something that cannot be found on any elite papyrus.

ARISTOTLE: (Silence)

POPULIST: Prove it. Prove to me that all humans are mortal.

ARISTOTLE: (Nervous smile)

POPULIST: See? You can't prove it. (Confident grin, a signature trait that will be exercised constantly to annoy Aristotle.) That's all right. What we understand from democracy is that all ideas can be represented in the public space, and they are respected equally. The gods say …

ARISTOTLE: This is not an idea, it's a fact. And we are talking about mortal humans.

POPULIST: If it were left up to you, you'd kill everybody to prove that all humans are mortal, just like your predecessors did.

ARISTOTLE: This is not going anywhere.

POPULIST: Please finish explaining your thinking, because I have important things to say.

ARISTOTLE: (Sigh) All humans are mortal. Socrates is a human …

POPULIST: I have to interrupt you there.

ARISTOTLE: Excuse me?

POPULIST: Well, I have to. These days, thanks to our leader, it is perfectly clear who Socrates is. We know very well who Socrates is! You cannot deceive us any more about that evil guy.

ARISTOTLE: Are you joking?

POPULIST: This is no joke to us, Mr Aristotle, as it may be to you. Socrates is a fascist. My people have finally realised the truth, the

54

real truth. The worm has turned. You cannot
deceive the people any more. You were going
to say, 'Therefore Socrates is mortal,' right?
We're fed up with your lies.

ARISTOTLE: You are rejecting the basics of logic.

POPULIST: I respect your beliefs.

ARISTOTLE: This is not a belief; this is logic.

POPULIST: I respect your logic, but you don't
respect mine. That's the main problem in
Greece today.

This is a simple example of the basic populist logic that,
with variations, is employed in many countries today.
However, even in this fictitious conversation there are
at least five fallacies according to the general rules of
rational debate, the fundamental rules of logic that we
have been using for centuries in everyday life, even if
we don't know any Latin:

1. *Argumentum ad hominem* (rebutting the
   argument by attacking the character of one's
   adversary rather than refuting the substance
   of the argument) – *You and your kind have
   ruled ...*

2. *Argumentum ad ignorantiam* (appealing to
   ignorance by asserting that a proposition is true
   because it has not yet been disproven) – *See?
   You can't prove that all humans are mortal.*

3. *Argumentum ad populum* (assuming that a proposition is true simply because many people believe it) – *The real people of this country think otherwise.*
4. *Reductio ad absurdum* (attempting to prove or disprove an argument by trying to show that it leads to an absurd conclusion) – *You'd kill everybody to prove that all humans are mortal.*
5. *Ad-hoc reasoning* (explaining why a certain thing *may* be by substituting an argument for why it *is*) – *Democracy is about respecting ideas, so respect my idea.*

Although the fallacies committed in the above conversation seem egregious, they did not appear childish to half of Britain when Boris Johnson and his ilk in the Conservative Party and the Leave campaign exercised them liberally during the Brexit debate. As Zoe Williams wrote in the *Guardian* on 16 October 2016: 'You'd hope for consistency and coherence; in its place, the bizarre spectacle of a party claiming to have been against the single market all along, because Michael Gove once said so.' In other words, *argumentum ad ignorantiam*. Michael Gove was the man who – bearing a striking resemblance to the populist driving Aristotle crazy above – declared that 'people in this country have had enough of experts'. It was comments like this that led the other half of Britain to believe that pro-Brexit arguments were too puerile to take seriously, and that only children could fall for them. Like millions of people in Europe, they also thought that if populist leaders were repeatedly portrayed as being childish, they would never be taken seriously enough to gain actual power.

'I will tell you one description that everyone [in the White House] gave – that everyone has in common. They all say he is like a child.'

Almost a year after the Brexit referendum, Americans were exercising the same 'adult strategy' on the other side of the Atlantic. When *Fire and Fury: Inside the Trump White House* was published in January 2018, its author Michael Wolff repeated this punchline in several TV interviews. The concerned nods of the composed presenters, together with Wolff's expression of someone bringing bad news, created the impression of a parent–teacher meeting being held to discuss a problem child. Each interview emphasised Trump's infantile behaviour, providing a comfortable underestimation of the situation for worried adult Americans. *He's just a wayward child, you know, and we are grown-ups. We know better.*

For any country experiencing the rise of populism, it's commonplace for the populist leader to be described as childlike. Reducing a political problem to the level of dealing with a naughty infant has a soothing effect, a comforting belittlement of a large problem. On 5 January 2018, the *New York Times* published a reader's letter that included the sentence: 'Looking at Thursday's headlines [on the war of words between Trump and his former chief strategist Steve Bannon] makes me wonder whether we have a government or a middle school student council.' The confidence of being the only adult in the room must have made the letter writer feel somehow secure. Just as the first minister of Wales, Carwyn Jones, must have felt on 15 November 2016, when he said, 'This is like giving a chainsaw to a child,' in response to Nigel Farage's name being put forward as someone who could help boost trade relations with Trump's America.

Portraying populist leaders as infantile is not the only trap that is all too easy to fall into. Scrutinising their childhoods to search for the traumas that must have turned them into such ruthless adults, and by doing so bandaging the political reality with some medical compassion that the populist leader didn't actually ask for, is another common ploy used by critics to avoid feeling genuine political anxiety. Poland's former populist prime minister Jarosław Kaczyński and Turkey's Erdoğan have both undergone such examinations *in absentia* by prominent psychiatrists, and have likewise been described as broken children. Elżbieta Sołtys, a Polish social scientist and psychologist, diagnosed

Kaczyński as a traumatised child. In one interview she said it was probable that his low emotional intelligence was connected to his loveless and strict upbringing, adding that his current fury was an explosion following years of suppression. Erdoğan's diagnosis was similar. His father used to hang him by his feet in order to stop him swearing, and as a result an entire country now has to suffer his volatile mood swings.

The primary consequence of calling these leaders infantile, and psychologising their ruthlessness, is simply to make their critics feel more adult and mentally healthy by comparison. It attributes childish politics entirely to the populist leader and his supporters. As if everyone else (including the writer of this book, and its readers) were completely immune to an infantilised perception of the world. *Well, it's not like that. You know that, right?*

'Why do you watch these films? These are just fairy tales for kids. You're grown men, goddamn it!'
It is 2016, and my friend Zeynep is talking to some Turkish male friends of ours in Istanbul. We are all in our forties, and the men she is reprimanding are all successful, upper-middle-class, well-educated. They have just finished playing fantasy football on the PlayStation, and are now trying to choose which movie to watch. Although they are the same age as the prophets and the revolutionary leaders of the last

century, with their backpacks dumped on the sofa
they look like adolescents just back from school. Their
political activity is limited to voting, mostly because
they consider politics beneath them. Of course they
are not as infantile as the people who believe a bigot
who keeps repeating the fairy tale of 'making Turkey
great again'. However, they do have a soft spot for
fairy tales; it's just that theirs involve vampires,
superpowers and Cristiano Ronaldo. As Zeynep
refuses to make light of the situation, the men first try
to fend off her attack with laughter, just as boys would.
But Zeynep insists: 'I mean, seriously. Why?' They
then choose to watch *The Hunger Games*, perhaps as
an attempt at conciliation, but she's still waiting for
a substantial answer, some sign of self-awareness or
self-criticism, as girls do. The men quickly move to
hawkish diplomacy. One of them, not jokingly, says,
'Well, you watch cartoon movies, don't you? You're
no better than us, *Mom*!'

Zeynep and I take our adult discussion into another
room. She talks about how infantile this generation
of men are, as millions of women surely do in countless other countries. And I start going on about Mark
Fisher's theory of capitalist realism, the ethical hege-
mony of 'That's the way the world is,' and the *depres-
sive hedonia* that comes with it. But then we start talking about how the new Lego movie is actually hilarious.
Later that night I think about the question of whether

the image of the 'good' leaders of our times is more adult than the 'evil' ones', or not.

'I drive an old Volkswagen because I don't need a better car.'

It's November 2015, and the former Uruguayan president José Mujica is speaking on stage. I'm chairing what will come to be remembered as an almost legendary talk to an audience of five thousand people, most of them not actually inside the congress building in Izmir, but outside watching on a giant screen. Mujica wants to talk about how Uruguay needs meat-cutting machines (because in order to be able to export its meat the country needs to be able to cut it in accordance with the regulations of other countries), but the audience seems to prefer the fun stuff: the cute old Beetle, his humble house, and so on. The next day, Mujica is described the same way in all the newspapers: 'The humblest of presidents who drives a Volkswagen Beetle and lives in a small house ...' There is no mention of him being a socialist, no ideological *blah blah*, none of the boring adult content. He is like Bernie Sanders, portrayed as the wise, cool old man during the Democratic primaries, or Jeremy Corbyn, whose home-made jam and red bicycle got more attention than his politics. These are the dervishes of our time, reduced to the kindly old men of fairy tales: fairy tales that attract those who see themselves as the adults and mock the 'infantile' supporters of populist leaders.

Much of the literature on populism and totalitarianism interprets the infantile narrative of the populists, as well as that of the 'deceived' masses who support them and choose to think in their fairy-tale language, as a political reaction that is specific to them. However, it would appear to be neither a reaction, nor specific. Rather, it's a coherent consequence of the times we live in, and something that contaminates all of us, albeit in different ways. Although it may seem that the current right-wing populist leaders are performing some kind of magic trick to mesmerise the previously rational adult masses and turn them into children, they aren't the ones who opened the doors to infantilised political language. The process started long before, when, in 1979, a famous handbag hit the political stage and the world changed.

That was the year a woman handbagged an entire nation with her black leather Asprey and said: 'There is no alternative.' When Margaret Thatcher 'rescued' a nation from the burden of having to think of alternatives, it resonated on the other side of the Atlantic with a man who perfected his presidential smile in cowboy movies. As the decade-long celebration of alternativelessness turned into a triumphalist neo-liberal disco dance on the remains of the Berlin Wall, the mainstream political vocabulary became a glitter-ball of words like 'vision', 'innovation', 'flexibility' and 'motivation', while gradually distancing itself from sepia, adult concepts like 'solidarity', 'equality' and 'social justice'. Because 'That's the way of the world.'

Meanwhile in Turkey, such terms, along with two hundred other 'leftist words', were officially banned from the state lexicon, and removed from the state TV channel, after the military coup in 1980. Whether through violence or neoliberalist persuasion, the mainstream vocabulary used globally to talk and think about the world and our place in it – regardless of what language we speak – was transformed into a sandpit for us to play safely in: socialism and fascism on opposite sides as the improbables of politics, religion and philosophy on the other sides as the irrelevants of ethics. Politics was reduced to mere administration, with people who knew about numbers and derivatives put in charge of taking care of us. It became the sort of bitter drink children would instinctively avoid, but if people did insist on having a taste, then bucketfuls of numbers were poured into their glasses to teach them a lesson. It is not surprising that Nigel Farage has said, 'I am the only politician keeping the flame of Thatcherism alive.' And although it angered many when Thatcher's biographer Jonathan Aitken said, 'I think she would have secretly cheered [Farage]' for his anti-refugee politics, it is nevertheless easy enough to picture Thatcher living down to her 1970s nickname by snatching milk out of the hands of Syrian children while saying, 'People must look after themselves first.' Ronald Reagan was likewise no less childlike when his team came up with the 'Let's make America great again' slogan for his election campaign in 1980.

The infantile political language of today, which seems to be causing a regression across the entire political spectrum, from right to left, is not in fact a reaction against the establishment, but instead something that follows the ideological fault lines of the establishment that was created in the eighties. The only significant difference between the forerunners and their successors – apart from the illusory economic boom that made the former look more upstanding than they actually were, and the response to the flood of refugees that makes the latter look even more unpleasant than they actually are – is that today the voice of populist infantile politics is amplified through social media, multiplying the fairy tales more than ever and allowing the ignorant to claim equality with the informed. They are, therefore, powerful enough this time around for there to be no limits to their attack on our capacity for political thought and basic reasoning. And we all now know that they are definitely less concerned with manners.

'The use of coarse language stresses that he is in tune with the man on the street. The debunking style, which often slides over the edge into insult, empha-

sizes his desire to distance himself from the political establishment.'*

Although this description would fit Trump, Erdoğan, Wilders and any other populist leader, it actually refers to Beppe Grillo, former comedian and the leader of the Italian Five Star movement. He is just another example of how the populists politicise so-called everyday language in order to establish a direct line of communication to the *real people*. Once this line is established the leader has lift-off, enabling him to appear not only to fly above politics, but as high as he wants to go: the sky is the limit. The perceived sincerity, or genuineness, of direct communication with the masses, and the image of the leader merging to become one with them, is a common political ritual of populism. Hugo Chávez did it every week on his personal TV show *Alo Presidente!*, Erdoğan has done it through his own media, Grillo performed the same stunt through his website, and Trump uses his famous tweets to have a heart-to-heart with his people, unfiltered by the *media elite*. The one important trick the populist leader has to pull off is that of making his supporters believe he is rejecting the elitist snobs and their media. He does so by including the media in his definition of 'the political

---

* Fabio Bordignon and Luigi Ceccarini, 'Five Stars and a Cricket: Beppe Grillo Shakes Italian Politics', *South European Society and Politics*, 21 February 2013.

elite', positioning it as an opponent – despite the fact that it is through the media that his connection to those masses is enabled.

This is a new political game that journalists are mostly unprepared for. It is a populist trick that Putin and Trump have both played on several occasions. On 7 July 2017, during the photo op before their one-on-one meeting at the G20 summit in Hamburg, Putin leaned towards Trump, gestured at the journalists in the room and asked, 'These the ones hurting you?' Trump did not hesitate to respond, 'These are the ones. You're right about that.' All at once it was as if the bully and the more established bully were preparing to take down some weaker kids in the playground. The journalists at the summit were shocked by this sudden and unprecedented switch of the spotlight. Not only were they themselves the story, they also found themselves portrayed as opponents on the political stage.

The supporters of both leaders no doubt enjoyed the moment, and relished the idea that a good wrestle – in either the American or the Russian style – was about to begin to knock out the spoiled media brats. Meanwhile the bewildered members of the press found themselves helplessly giggling and dancing around the ring in their efforts to avoid the attacks.

* * *

The global media probably wouldn't have been interested in what Thailand's prime minister, Prayuth Chanocha, had to say at a press conference on 9 January 2018 had he not put a lifesize cardboard cut-out of himself in front of a microphone and told the assembled journalists to 'Put your questions to this guy.' He then left the venue with a swagger, the very image of the jolly populist leader who had already achieved a lot, and it wasn't even midday yet. The journalists were left smiling awkwardly, as if a child had just done something outrageous and there was nothing the adults present could do but hide their embarrassment by laughing. The BBC used the same type of laughter in a trailer that shows Trump heckling a BBC reporter – 'Here's another beauty' – at a press conference while the other journalists present smile with raised eyebrows like intimidated adults in the school playground. Erdoğan does it in a more Middle Eastern macho style, occasionally reprimanding the members of his own media, jokingly treating them like little rascals, but *his* little rascals, live on air, at which they giggle obediently every time.

Numerous critics and analysts believe that by displaying such rudeness, populist leaders reject the notion that the media plays an integral role in democracy. However, looking at different examples around the globe, it seems that this ostentatious offensiveness is actually a requirement to establish direct communication between the leader and the masses. Furthermore, it is not actually a rejection of the media at all, but is rather a means of embracing and using them. The question of whether journalists are capable of refusing to play the role assigned to them and defending their personal and institutional dignity is another story, one that will be discussed in the next chapter. Suffice to say, there can be no doubt that they serve as a whipping boy who must be beaten whenever a display of 'These are my people and I don't give a damn what the establishment write about us' is required. The leader does not even have to talk about the hideous nature of *loser* Socrates; dismissing *oppressive* Aristotle serves well enough.

'It's like making a milkshake without the lid on,' wrote a Turkish Twitter user, trying to describe the impossibility of having a proper political discussion with Erdoğan supporters. The guy had evidently been subjected to more seasoned versions of the populist logic and debating tactics than in our earlier Aristotle conversation, which are far harder to pin down. They vary from *whataboutism* to an ever-shifting ground of contradictory arguments; from bringing up the utterly irrelevant to being proudly inconsistent. And when the logic begins to feel like milkshake dripping down the wall, it seems there are only two ways to go: the French way or the American way.

On 4 May 2017, *La Dépêche du Midi*, a newspaper based in Toulouse, described the decisive presidential election debate between Marine Le Pen and Emmanuel Macron as 'revelatory'. The article continued: 'Through lies and incessant interruptions, striking proof was provided last night that it is difficult, if not impossible, to debate with the far right in conditions of such minimal democratic respect.' The French preferred to leave the mess of the milkshake well alone, presumably because they are more familiar with Albert Camus, who once said: 'A man with whom one cannot reason is a man to be feared.'

The American media, by contrast, having more humility than their French counterparts, published some articles that did at least attempt to *know better* than the infantile Trumpeteers. Paul Thagard, Professor of Philosophy and Cognitive Science at Canada's Waterloo University, said to Nadya Apraval in an interview for the Popsugar website that if one wants to change a Trump supporter's mind, one should 'look for common ground or shared values'. However, when vulgarity and ignorance become esteemed values, what do you do? How can you communicate with a person if he embraces his leader's hypocrisy and inconsistency as a tactic performed for the good of his people?

While the public mind is grappling with these fundamental questions (questions that not only shake the rationale behind, but also the basic consensus of, good manners), the populist movement busies itself with recruiting intellectuals and opinion-makers who are far more eloquent than the interlocutor who so wrongfooted Aristotle earlier in this chapter. These new recruits would have plunged Aristotle into gloom at the realisation that they are his peers, members of his own Academy, educated adults, and not the philistines of Athens. Some of them might even be people he calls friends.

His features wouldn't look so 'rural' if his glasses were less ostentatiously hip. His accent wouldn't sound so 'provincial' were his boldness not so inflammatory and vulgar. He sports a moderate-Islamist, *nouveau riche* suit, and a huge Ottoman ring that must have worked before on the women of his acquaintance, for he cannot stop playing with it. Although he has begged for this appointment for about a year, and has been turned down numerous times, he speaks with a certain impatience, as if he is too busy to spare time for me: a well-practised business-world attitude aimed at damaging the self-esteem of others. We are in one of Istanbul's hip cafés in the summer of 2006, and I just sit there and listen, not only because the conversation disgusts me to the bone, but also because he never stops talking, as if to remind me how important he is and what great influence *the movement* has over the media. My blank expression is obviously mistaken for approval, as he gradually becomes more blunt, until finally he comes to the heart of the matter.

'So, to cut to the chase, you write good things about us in your column, and we help you in return. We know you very well. We know that you are not interested in money or promotion, but ... Well, let me put it this way: a group from the movement will be going to southern Africa for an official visit, and only one journalist will have an interview with Desmond Tutu, if you know what I mean.'

His clumsy, mafia grin paralyses me, and I just say 'Oh?' which he apparently takes as an invitation to elaborate, so he goes a little deeper.

'As you already know, this movement is not really about religion. To be frank, I too look at women and girls.'

At this point he lowers his gaze to my breasts, grinning as though this is some kind of groundbreaking libertarian statement.

'This is about power and money. Well, you already know that. You keep writing about it all the time. Ha ha ha ... So, as I said before – you support us and we help you, if you know what I mean.'

Poor guy, he is simply incapable of anticipating what is going to happen.

'How dare you! How dare you!' I shout, pounding the table. Heads turn towards us as his body shrinks into his shiny suit and back to his provincial roots; back to the time before the ruling party furnished him with power.

I tend to repeat myself when enough disgust and fury have boiled up inside me. So before storming out of the café, I shout it one more time: 'How dare you!'

From this point on, beginning the very next day, I become an object of obsession for government-supporting papers and websites. For ten years and more I'm the evil woman with a thousand faces. One day I'm an Iranian spy, another I'm the concubine of a Saudi sheikh; one day I'm betraying the country by conspiring with *devious Brits* or *treacherous Germans*, the next I'm single-handedly organising the Gezi uprising, travelling to the capital to speak to alien enemies, 'on flight TK 768, seat 7C'. When they cannot come up with something creative, or are unable to track me close enough to know my seat number on the plane, they just put some irrelevant content on Twitter with an outrageous heading about me, confident that hardly anyone will actually read the tweet itself, but that the slur will stick if repeated often enough.

So, if nothing else, my experience with the stooge in the café, and the years of written and verbal abuse that followed, helped me to understand how a populist right-wing movement attempts to drag left-wing intellectuals onto its side to form temporary alliances that legitimise it in the eyes of a wider audience. There is no sophistication, no subtlety, not much in the way of intellectual content. As a famous Turkish football coach once said: 'No tactics! Bam bam bam!' I'd always imagined the process would follow some kind of secret-services-recruitment protocol, but it is actually as cheap and repugnant as any dirty bargain. The movement's representatives, a human resources department of sorts, ask for an appointment, you sit at a table, they talk the small-time mafia talk, you take the deal, and your life suddenly becomes prosperous – or not, in which case you find yourself having to tell people that you're not a sex slave in a Saudi palace, in fact you're in Tahrir Square following the protests.

The café encounter took place at a time when Erdoğan and his party were basking in praise from both inside and outside the country, so it would not have been quite as embarrassing as it would have been in later years for me to have accepted such a pact, to have left the table with a handshake rather than a shout, and then seen my face adorning billboards as I was heralded as a star opinion-maker. For some, the justification for making such an alliance lay in shared resentment of the army's strong-arm administration. For others it was enthusiasm for re-establishing Turkey's ties with Middle Eastern countries. Others perhaps believed that co-operating might bring about a solution to the Kurdish conflict, or have trusted in the new, liberal constitution that Erdoğan *personally* promised. For all these reasons, and more, it was easy for opinion-makers to convince themselves that Erdoğan was simply a strong leader in need of a little support from *proper adults*, and some educated advice – in other words, *their* advice. They became the *wise men* of the time, and being invited onto Erdoğan's plane to enjoy the lukewarm glow of basking in the prince's favour was sufficient reward. Maybe some of them applied their higher political theory to the *realpolitik* of the day and, on an intellectual level, genuinely believed that once the oppressed *real people* were given their voice they would become active agents of a liberal democracy. They may also have believed that the politicised provincialism would be respectful of the rights of others once they were given the chance to lead their provincial lifestyles to the full.

But in general terms, these commentators all took part in a political game in which they overestimated themselves. When the populist party started to colonise the judicial system, and army generals were prosecuted with false allegations, I was talking to one of the newly-aligned newspaper columnists, who had been a prominent leftist opinion leader since the seventies. 'This is dangerous,' I said. 'They're politicising the already crippled legal system, and you're supporting this process. Aren't you afraid this might come back to haunt you in the end?'

He was at least twenty-five years older than me, and he proceeded to offer me a few life lessons. 'Well, sweetie, let's get rid of these army bastards first, then we'll deal with Erdoğan.'

'But how? With whose support? With what power?' I asked.

He gave me that patronising, compassionate smile every young woman knows only too well, and said, 'You are so naïve, my dear. This is politics. You make alliances. And then you make new alliances.'

In a short while he was given his own talk show on state TV.

A few years later, however, almost all the intellectuals who'd supported Erdoğan either sought exile in other European countries or ended up in prison. Some of them managed to reinvent themselves in Western countries as *deceived* members of the opposition, making new alliances to carry on their careers abroad as the spectacular victims of the spectacular dictator. And the stooge in the café who had offered me a prosperous future, having once been a prominent figure in the Gülen movement, Erdoğan's closest allies for a long time, became an *enemy of the real people*, hunted down internationally by the president. He disappeared. Because this is politics, *sweetie*, and Erdoğan made new alliances, *if you know what I mean*.

Maybe someone should mention these fallen petit Machiavellians to the CNN presenter Fareed Zakaria, who on 7 April 2017 declared joyously, upon learning that the US had bombed Syria, 'Trump has become the president tonight!' Or to the journalist and author Jonah Goldberg, who was a strong Republican critic of Trump before the election, but changed his tune after the inauguration, saying that '[Trump] has to get our approval on the important things,'* ignoring the fact that the new president might not feel the need to ask for advice. Or to Thomas Friedman, the *New York Times* columnist who likened Trump's election to Pearl Harbor and 9/11 before becoming supportive just because he liked the idea of limiting immigration with a wall. Or to the late Nobel Prize-winning playwright Dario Fo, who supported a populist like Beppe Grillo because he believed Italy needed 'a surreal fantasist'.

Similar cynicism has been voiced by several of today's European intellectuals, who intellectualise the insanity in the name of shaking up the *corrupt establishment*, and blame other intellectuals for being *out of touch with reality* and *real people*. This is an easy trick to pull off when the rational few are having to face off against millions of surreal fantasists, and are already doubting themselves anyway, forever asking themselves the question, 'Am I out of touch?'

On 30 November 2016, the DR Concert Hall in Copenhagen was filled with six hundred high-profile international journalists, but it was as silent as a graveyard. Nigel Farage, keynote speaker at the

---

* Kelefa Sanneh, 'Intellectuals for Trump', *New Yorker*, 9 January 2017.

NewsXChange symposium, was so delighted that it wasn't him but the audience that was dying, that he called out, 'Cheer up! This is not a funeral!'

Nobody cheered up. By the time Farage started his jubilant presentation on the already-defeated title of the symposium, 'Are We Out of Touch?', the sarcastic smirks that had been present before the Brexit referendum and the US election had been replaced by stiff upper lips and the realisation that it was not a single man, but millions who were flying the same flag. In the face of the silence of the journalists, Farage was free to enjoy himself, and he commenced by saying how desperately out of touch the press was with real people, and proceeding to graciously offer them a lesson in journalism.

Conventional counter-attacks by the panellists and distinguished members of the audience followed, but they failed to box Farage and his narrative into a corner. The tools they used were those adopted by many to expose the truth about such political figures: fact-checking, holding him to account, promoting constructive journalism, and trying to embarrass Farage and wipe the grin off his face by calling him a liar and a xenophobe.

As one of the panellists, I smiled bitterly as I thought about how all these brilliant journalists were yet to suffer the despair of realising that their tactics were akin to playing chess against a pigeon, as someone once described debating evolution with a creationist: the pigeon will just knock over all the pieces and shit on the board, then depart, proudly claiming victory and leaving the mess behind for you to clean up. It's no coincidence that Garry Kasparov, the former world chess champion, left Russia to live abroad after playing an excruciating game with Putin.

When Farage departed, announcing, as if trying to get away from a deadly boring party, that he was off to Washington to meet Donald Trump, hundreds of journalists had only just begun two long days of flagellating themselves over how out of touch they were.

They didn't know that a second, decisive attack was still to come: the humiliation, mocking and discrediting of prominent public figures, intellectuals and journalists. The witch-burning had yet to commence.

When you're Meryl Streep and a president like Trump calls you 'overrated', Robert De Niro and George Clooney, two bastions of cool, can come to your rescue and turn the humiliating attack into a global joke. However, for the rest of us, who have less handsome friends, or who are faced with a populist leader who knows it's better to start the whole discrediting process by targeting weaker public figures, it feels as if we're engaged in a sword fight with ghosts.

In 2012, online harassment wasn't yet a 'thing'. So when I responded to a massive social media attack by tweeting 'The government has waged a war against opposing public figures with its troll army. Women journalists, including me, are particularly being targeted,' the response was yet more mocking: 'Oh! You think you are that important ah?' 'Oh, now she goes all paranoid.' I realised I was caught in a virtual loop from which a *real* person with normal emotional responses cannot escape, and that trying to match my abusers' sarcasm and irony with my own would hit a dead-end, because – as we will see in later chapters – they can always top your sarcasm with vulgarity.

Four years later, Swedish TV presenter Alexandra Pascalidou apparently felt the same thing when she told the *Sydney Morning Herald* on 24 November 2016: 'Some say switch it off, it's just online. It doesn't count. But it does count, and it's having a real impact on our lives. Hate hurts. And it often fuels action IRL [in real life].' This is one of the reasons why, in 2016, as populist politics started to contaminate Australian politics, the female journalists of the country joined forces to campaign against online abuse. That same year, the International Press Institute produced a report on 'Countering Online Abuse of Female Journalists'. The issue has since been brought to the European Union's attention, with a demand for new regulations to be put in place. However, even if adequate laws are passed, and even if you're prepared to dedicate your entire life to bringing the authors of each of the hundreds of thousands of abusive tweets to court, how do you get to the root of such shamelessness?

While dissident public figures are under siege from never-ending white noise, the debate also becomes clogged up by newly invented concepts conjured up by the movement's opinion and commentary leaders, such as 'neighbourhood pressure',* 'anxious seculars',† or Trump's label for Democrats, 'obstructionist losers'.‡ As critical media and opposition voices are circumvented via a bombardment from populist opinion-makers, the new concepts trickle down to the troll armies and get simplified, multiplied and used as ammunition to colonise the political communications sphere. Soon afterwards, communication chaos takes over, transforming the way intellectuals speak and turning them into semantic street-fighters. Intellectual activity becomes a matter of reacting to fragments of populist discourse with sarcasm, in an attempt to combat them with their own weapons. The language of political debate is reduced to the cage-fighting level, where anything is

---

* A concept used to label opposition voices, arguing that critical intellectuals are influenced only by their own circles.

† A label that was used in Turkey to imply that dissident intellectuals suffered from Islamophobia and were paranoid about an Islamic republic.

‡ Trump used the label during the US government shutdown in January 2018.

allowed, until even the most prominent intellectuals are dancing to the populists' tune.

'I'm not sure that what we're doing can still be called intellectual work,' said one of my friends (who wants to remain anonymous in this book). It was the winter of 2018, and he was complaining that despite being a popular political columnist who was frequently invited on to television political discussions, this did not mean that people actually read or listened to what he wrote or said. He was convinced that his readers and social media followers were more interested in whether his angry sentences struck the right note in response to the populist discourse. 'As long as you use the same adolescent cynicism and use the same fighting techniques, the readers and the audience don't give a damn whether your words have substance or not. They simply want you to win because you're their fighter in the cage, and that's it.'

A few months after our exchange with Özgür Mumcu, the cage fight he talked about became a global matter thanks to Donald Trump's former strategist and the rock star of the alt-right, Steve Bannon, and the high-profile invitations he received. The *Economist*'s Open Future Festival in London, the *New Yorker* Festival, the NewsXchange Festival in Edinburgh and the Oxford Union invited him to debates. The invitations aroused many protests, and other prominent guests cancelled their appearances. The intellectual giants were split between the urge to defeat the beast of right-wing populism in a cage fight, and seeming to be placed on the same level as him by appearing on the same stage. Some organisations cancelled their scheduled fights due to the protests, while others, including the Oxford Union, insisted that fascism is just another idea in the free market of ideas, and that it can be refuted by rational argument.

Regardless of what took place at these events, Bannon's was the only name that stuck in people's minds, leaving the other reluctant or enthusiastic participants with tainted or faded reputations. More importantly, the mainstream intellectual sphere was filled with discussion about whether Bannon and his ilk should be fought on 'our' turf or not – thus transforming that turf into merely the setting for a fruitless and impossible dispute. Meanwhile Bannon was presented with the priceless badge of being 'the man who single-handedly terrorised the entire intellectual establishment in Europe'.

As the prominence of progressive intellect is gradually reduced to point-scoring against an opponent on social media or on the TV screen, the question of respectability becomes a problem for the critics of populism. Meanwhile, as the populist movement gains in power, the number of intellectuals lining up alongside the populist leaders rises – not because supporting them becomes less embarrassing, but because it has become

normal. This is why Donald Trump received a standing ovation from Congress for his State of the Union
address in January 2018, something that would have
seemed unimaginable to many Congress members only
a year before, when he first entered the White House.

The power of numerical normality encourages
further departures from rationality, and expands the
limits of vulgarity until it has invaded the entire public
sphere. One hardly realises how dire the damage to free
thought and free speech is until the day comes when,
for example, an important petition against the populist leader is launched, and you find yourself struggling
to come up with prominent names who have not been
tainted by the cage fight or driven crazy by the chaos.
And in the end you come up with none. The critical
voice becomes orphaned in the public sphere, and the
opposing masses become a silent ship adrift without
a lighthouse as they lose their opinion leaders. Their
desperation deepens as they realise that the centrifuge
of the dominant narrative has sucked in those they
believed knew better. At the same time, the populist
media discourse is amplified and repeated to such a
degree that even opposing elements of society begin to
lose track of its serial crimes against rationality. That's
when you find yourself, finally, too exhausted to say,
'Well, *it didn't happen like that. You know that, right?*'

There is no law to prevent right-wing populist
political language invading and destroying the public

sphere. Therefore, when dissident voices become choked with anger, exhausted by the tireless attacks of party apparatchiks and maddened by the slipperiness of the ever-changing populist discourse, their last resort becomes begging for simple ethical manners, and shouting in the street or on social media, 'Have some decency!' And at one point this might have worked, too.

'Have you left no sense of decency?' asked the American lawyer Joseph Welch on 9 June 1954. Welch was serving as the chief counsel for the United States Army, which was under investigation for communist activities in the Army–McCarthy Senate hearings, and in one of the televised sessions Senator Joseph McCarthy launched an attack on a young man employed in Welch's Boston law office. As an amazed television audience looked on, Welch responded with the immortal lines that ultimately ended McCarthy's career: 'Until this moment, Senator, I think I have never really gauged your cruelty or your recklessness.' When McCarthy tried to continue his attack, Welch angrily interrupted, 'Let us not assassinate this lad further, Senator. You've done enough. Have you no sense of decency, sir?' After a four-year-long communist witch-hunt, Welch's question led to the evaporation of McCarthy's popularity virtually overnight.

However, those times are over. The world has altered dramatically since Joseph Welch changed American history simply by asking a question. And over the last decades the veins of rationality have become swollen with fury from calling – to no avail – for shame, while the populist has simply widened his grin and taken pride in his victory. We have finally lost what Albert Camus called 'the old confidence [that] man had in himself, which led him to believe that he could always elicit human reactions from another man if he spoke to him in the language of a common humanity'. And so it is no wonder that more and more people are surrendering to the weariness of the child who just wants to get to the end of the tale and go to sleep.

THREE

Remove the Shame: Immorality is 'Hot' in the Post-Truth World

In autumn 2017, Turkey all of a sudden became abuzz with a new *scientific* theory from an AKP youth organisation member. His article on the party website argued that the earth is in fact flat, and that the theory of a spherical world is a conspiracy forced on the real people by the Vatican, Zionists, Freemasons and various other evil powers. The next day, dozens of articles in government-supporting newspapers appeared explaining the philosophical grounding of the article, and all of them ultimately shared the same conclusion: that science is just one narrative among many, just another truth. The government trolls merely had to broadcast this absurd idea on social media for it to trickle down into the debate. In a matter of hours, thousands of trolls and energised fools were shouting out, in a revolutionary manner, against oppressive scientists, and protesting at the cruel dominance of science. The maddening arrogance of the ignorant was having another fiesta; one of many since their leader Erdoğan, who thinks evolution is 'just a theory' which we don't have to take too seriously, came to power. And once again, many Turkish citizens, bewildered by the limitless confidence of the ignorant, were desperately trying to remain polite while attempting to defend the singleness of truth.

Several months later, on 21 February 2018, and 'It is –' said seventeen-year-old David Hogg, then paused to find the right word, before eventually choosing 'incredible.' He was one of the survivors of the mass shooting at Marjory Stoneman Douglas High School in Florida that had taken place seven days earlier, and which had cost the lives of seventeen students and staff. Now he was appearing on CNN International, responding to a troll attack that claimed the shooting was a hoax, and he himself was merely an actor. After he had voiced concerns about gun violence, it took only a few days for American trolls to place him in the defendant's chair. David Hogg found himself having to prove that he was not acting on behalf of the anti-gun lobby, and that his former FBI agent father had not coached him to speak out against Donald Trump. And finally, cornered by the barrage of untruths, he was even being forced to prove that he really was a student at the school, which he had thought until then was an unquestionable fact, like the roundness of the earth.

In recent years, countless people in several countries have found themselves in a similar position, having to defend the truth against those who just don't feel like believing them. The most bitter battles over basic communication became routine, first on social media and then on TV screens. There were no rules of war to regulate behaviour in these battles, and the looters of the truth rampaged unconstrained. Lies that they rebranded as 'alternative facts' multiplied at such a speed that it was as if there were an all-you-can-eat buffet from which you could simply pick and choose what you wished to believe. While the defenders of truth looked on helplessly, the looters were unembarrassed as they piled their plates high with made-up stories, groundless ideas and theories that showed no regard for common sense or centuries of long-accumulated knowledge. And in 2016 when Oxford Dictionaries finally gave this mess a name – 'post-truth' – we entered a new age. Or so many believed.

Lies, and the replacement of truth with nonsense, are in fact as old as storytelling. It probably goes back to that smarty-pants *Homo sapiens* who drew himself single-handedly killing the largest mammoth with a spear, when he had actually stayed behind in the cave enjoying his new set of charcoals while the real hunters were outside trying to bring home the bacon. And when humans first discovered how easy it was to rewrite history, which coincided with the invention of writing in Babylon, there was no going back. From then on, the rulers owned the magical power of the word, and since the lions couldn't tell their own story, we kept hearing the one that glorifies the hunter, as the African proverb goes. Therefore, in 2016, when Oxford Dictionaries chose it as their word of the year, 'post-truth' was already old news to lions, to women, to children, and to all those deemed powerless, dehumanised, outcast, and ignored. For thousands of years they have been asking the astonished question that has become the chorus of our current times: 'But how can they say that?!' This time, however, the victim is different. The established and the powerful are now having a taste of what it feels like to be subjected to shameless lies. The truth is no longer a deer on the king's estate, to be killed only by those who sit on the throne.

Unfortunately, as the age-old monopoly of creating the truth was weakening, the authority of science, common sense and basic moral consensus were all looted by the ignorant as well. They were the spoils of the warriors in this new war between the established leaders of liberal democracy and the new warlords, the right-wing populist leaders. In an age of anything goes, the looters were allowed, and in fact encouraged, by their leaders to attack anything that the old world deemed good and right – from participatory democracy to the fact that the earth is round, or the consensus that children should not be killed in schools. The cavalry of troll armies led the campaign of 'useful idiots' who were already exulting in their newly discovered power. Like the cruel Babylonian ruler Hammurabi, who enjoyed the privilege of writing that he was 'the king of Justice', authoritarian leaders presented themselves to the masses as the real democrats. Eventually the armies of 'alternative truth' became strong enough to change political realities through lies, and to build what felt like new countries out of nonsense. When panic finally seized the political sphere – when made-up statistics such as 'Muslims will reproduce to become the majority in Europe in ten years', or insanely ignorant conspiracy theories, multiplied to become more powerful than grounded analysis – it became easy to forget that it was the kings of recent times who had prepared the ground for these crimes against truth.

The spectre of alternative truth – highly organised, large-scale lies – that haunts the establishment today was heralded by the normalisation of shamelessness. And this organised shamelessness, when it made its first appearance on the face of the earth, was accompanied by one of the most dramatic spectacles in human history. One night in January 1991 we turned on our

TVs and, as we watched, an earthquake took place that changed the shape of our hearts.

In August that year, people all over the world were hypnotised by the Scud missiles flying over Christiane Amanpour's head as she reported live on the allied invasion of Iraq for CNN. All of a sudden it was morally OK to talk about how thrilling the technological breakthrough was that allowed us to watch a war on live TV. A real bombardment in a real country became a spectacle for viewers around the world, whereas only nineteen years earlier, in 1972, a single photo from the Vietnam War had been enough for thousands of American people to take to the streets to express their moral outrage. Nick Ut's picture of a naked Vietnamese girl, her flesh melting as she flees a napalm attack, was taken in a black-and-white world when the good and the bad, the beautiful and the ugly were not yet blurred, let alone replaced by their opposites. This was why President Nixon would try to prevent the publication of the photo, fearing the public reaction. By contrast, only two decades later Big Media was proudly broadcasting the war in Iraq 24/7, knowing that images of dying children would no longer generate either such shame or such outrage.

Thus began an enormous shift in the tectonic plates of the human perception of evil. A crack opened in the mainland of truth, splitting it into separate islands of reality. We as humanity were no longer sharing the same one truth, which meant that other people's tragedies didn't necessarily generate an emotional response within our personal island of reality. Our perception of evil started evolving in such a way that the good old 'dehumanisation of the enemy' was no longer even required; the suffering of the other was simply irrelevant.

Then, after the first Iraq war came the war in the former Yugoslavia. Only five decades after the Second World War, in this new world it took yet another genocide and images of new concentration camps before shame intervened and people were finally forced to acknowledge the horror occurring on other people's 'islands'. It was actually then that the term 'post-truth' was used for the first time. In 1992 Steve Tesich, in an article for *The Nation*, wrote:

> We are rapidly becoming prototypes of a people that totalitarian monsters could only drool about in their dreams. All the dictators up to now have had to work hard suppressing the truth. We, by our actions, are saying that it is no longer necessary, that we have acquired a spiritual mechanism that can denude truth of any significance. In a very fundamental way we, as a free people, have freely decided that we want to live in some post-truth world.

This was a time when the prefix 'post' was quite trendy, 'post-ideology' being the most fashionable use of it. And it was probably too early for Tesich to see that being blinded to the facts or the truth was not necessarily a free choice made by free people. Rather it was a forced mutation of the human mind to make it comply with the new moral set-up of our times, where shame and mercy became the responsibility of the individual, and no longer the business of political institutions.

The beginning of the end, the irreversible separation of the mainland of truth into islands of separate realities, came with the Western attacks on Afghanistan following 9/11. Only weeks after the first bombardment in 2001, CNN International began promoting Afghanistan as a tourist destination for those who wanted to enjoy *real* excitement. Presumably this was part of a reconstruction programme, begun prematurely, intended to make the country an extreme sports destination after the war. Apparently there was nothing immoral in planning your vacation on an island in someone else's reality just because it was inconveniently filled with dead bodies. In later years, the idea of cruising around the islands of other people's bloody realities was to become so normal that on 3 October 2017, Britain's then foreign secretary Boris Johnson was able to say complacently that the Libyan city of Sirte could become 'the next Dubai', while adding a bit of tourism advice: 'The only thing they've got to do is clear the dead bodies away.'

After Afghanistan, since the islands of realities were already separate, it was possible to widen the gap and push the limits of creating new 'truths'. On 5 February 2003, American secretary of state Colin Powell held up a little tube filled with colourful fluid at a meeting of the United Nations Security Council in New York. He started talking about centrifuges, uranium, nuclear facilities – and the next thing you know, bombs were raining down on Baghdad again. The mental and moral transformation that enabled this monumental post-truth operation was revealed in 2004 in the *New York Times* magazine. In Ron Suskind's piece there was a quote from an anonymous aide to President George W. Bush: 'The aide said that guys like me were "in what we call the reality-based community", which he defined as people who "believe that solutions emerge from your judicious study of discernible reality ... That's not the way the world really works any more," he continued. "We're an empire now, and when we act, we create our own reality. And while you're studying that reality – judiciously, as you will – we'll act again, creating other new realities, which you can study too, and that's how things will sort out. We're history's actors ... and you, all of you, will be left to just study what we do."' *Just a perfect day in the cave* for enjoying the new charcoal set ...

* * *

This was the last time that those humans mockingly described as 'reality-based' expressed *en masse* their rejection of the splitting of reality and attempted to keep the fragmented islands of humanity together. Worldwide protests formed the biggest anti-war demonstration in human history. We didn't know then that the 'No to War' slogans swaying in every capital city around the world were actually dancing to the swansong of morality in global politics. Despite the epic support it received, the Stop the War Coalition failed in every country but one – Turkey. When the peace movement there managed to stop the government from joining the coalition, as one of two spokespeople for the movement, I proudly celebrated this feat in my column, much to the disapproval of disappointed pro-war columnists who wrote about the 'missed opportunity', using business parlance and vehemently blaming people like me for being childish. According to the already fully-fledged new dominant moral set-up, we, the people who had felt too ashamed to be part of a merciless campaign, were now supposed to feel embarrassed for not understanding what they kept calling *realpolitik*. The new reality was that war was fair and good. Thus we became the lions of the African proverb.

It was around this time that the practice of splitting the TV screen into two or more windows during news broadcasts became more widespread globally. One of them would show the live war footage, uninterrupted, while the other showed the talking heads, some preaching about *realpolitik* with lusty elaborations on the power of modern weaponry, while others, invited into the studio to represent the other 'truth', attempted to remind viewers that real human lives were involved. Meanwhile, a stock exchange stream ribbon might be running across the bottom of the screen, as if it were natural to show the profit and loss caused by the footage being shown. This divided perception of a catastrophe added another layer to our shame, but the Nasdaq opening bell was louder than any human voice as it celebrated war profits right from the first bombardment.

The Stop the War protests marked the last time that the masses, acting upon their vicarious shame, believed that their protest would change politics once the *real people* were told the truth. It may have been because we were the last generation brought up with the conviction that shame and mercy are to be valued, rather than being evidence of an embarrassing naïveté that obstructs the vision of the *real*. The words of Primo Levi, the Italian writer who survived Auschwitz, were still fresh for us: 'It was not possible for us, nor did we want, to become islands – the just among us, neither more or less numerous than in any other human group, felt remorse, shame and pain for the misdeeds that others and not they had committed, and in which they felt involved, because they sensed that what had happened around them in their presence, and in them, was irrevocable.'* After all, ours may also have been the last generation to be reprimanded for being shameless when we turned a blind eye to suffering.

'Look at those kids! They don't have anything to eat, and you're playing with your food!'

For people like me who grew up in the seventies and eighties, Somalia and Ethiopia were not so much distant countries hit by disasters and droughts as a means to feel ashamed at having plenty, a reference parents used to reprimand children who didn't finish their meals. The starving children were neither the extras in an abstract humanitarian crisis, nor a 'disturbing image' TV audiences need to be warned about, as they have become today. They were our less fortunate siblings, with whom we shared the same womb of truth and whom we were supposed to look at and learn lessons from. Those dying children lived permanently inside our heads, inside our single truth, at our dinner tables, not in some too distant to be relevant continent. Our mothers were not yet capable of imagining a world where people might keep their children away from such images just because they might upset them. By contrast, in September 2015, editors in newsrooms around the

---

* Primo Levi, *The Drowned and the Saved* (Simon & Schuster, 1988).

world were asking themselves whether photos of Aylan Kurdi, a three-year-old Syrian boy whose body washed up on the Aegean coast, should be published or not. Their hesitation was caused not only by the fact that the images were so disturbing, but also because we all knew by then that showing images of senseless human tragedy would probably have no consequence. People wouldn't take to the streets in vicarious shame to try to change the course of history, although they might indulge in a lot of angry condemnation via hashtags. However, what was to happen in Hungary only a few days later would prove shocking even to those of us who understood all too well the new rules of shame, mercy and the division of realities.

While the world was still deeply disturbed by the photos of the drowned boy, on the Hungarian border a camerawoman named Petra László was photographed enthusiastically kicking another Syrian refugee child. But the most surprising part of this story was yet to come. One year later, in October 2016, we learned that László was in fact deeply sensitive to the refugee issue, when she received an award for a film she had made about the Hungarian refugees of 1956. The Hungarian government spokesperson who presented the award, just like child-kicking Petra László, could see no moral contradiction in this story. When asked by a reporter about the hypocritical situation during the award ceremony, the spokesperson replied, 'No. The Hungarian refugees of 1956 are not the same as today's migrants.' The mutation of human perception that made possible the division of realities had been so successful that the question of morality had become irrelevant. And this shameless behaviour was not only possible in the twenty-first century, but might very well have been seen as 'hot'.

'That's hot!'

In the groundbreaking reality TV show *The Simple Life*, which ran from 2003 to 2007, Paris Hilton and Nicole Richie, two super-rich American socialites, visited poor people's lives to explore other realities. Their catchphrase was 'That's hot!' although mostly the lives they were discovering were 'so not hot'. In one of the episodes, when the duo get on a bus for the first time in their lives, an old man tells them he has just been to a funeral. Hilton's response is brief: 'That's hot.' The blonde duo's detachment from, and sometimes disgust at, other disenfranchised realities was so amusing to the audience that many did not realise that this touristic cruise around other people's lives was not so different in essence from their own viewing of guided missiles arcing over Baghdad. *The Simple Life* first appeared on our screens in the same year as the Second Gulf War – and it was around then that we transformed from citizens who acted out of shame and were inclined to show mercy into reality TV audiences with brains adapted to navigate the new archipelago of truth.

Paris Hilton was right when she said, 'I don't think there's ever been anyone like me that's lasted. And I'm going to keep on lasting.' Her legacy would only flourish with time. Just a few years later, overstepping the new limits of shamelessness and exhibiting detachment from other people's realities would prove a profitable attitude. Not only detachment from, but actually laughing at, the less fortunate became an industry, and countless web channels were spawned, their comic material made up of non-stop videos of people injuring themselves. On TV reality shows, small, isolated groups of people made each other suffer, or even watched the losers starve, as in *Survivor*. The industry found no shortage of ambitious collaborators eager to show what humans are capable of when shame and mercy are removed from the list of ground rules.

This new type of entertainment created a new kind of human, an audience not necessarily entertained, but definitely mesmerised, by immorality, who over time became almost addicted to witnessing cruelty. The worst representatives of humankind became the stars of this new morality, and humanity was happy to shift its moral orbit to revolve around them. After all, watching these shows, witnessing their contempt for human dignity, no longer meant that you had to share the same reality as the victims. No vicarious shame was required.

It was easy to disconnect your empathy. So much so that by 2018 disconnectedness had become a proud personal manifesto for another woman, equally blonde as Hilton and Richie, but not quite as much of a joke. In April that year, Katie Hopkins probably felt rather 'hot' when she wrote in her *Sun* column: 'NO, I don't care. Show me pictures of coffins, show me bodies floating in water, play violins and show me skinny people looking sad. I still don't care.' Feeling nothing was now a badge of honour.

Eventually, what started out as a blonde-girl joke ended up teaching us that you could even become the president of the United States if you performed shamelessness and detachment with sufficient brazenness. Donald Trump's stardom was born through the ultimate act of rejecting mercy, by excommunicating the weak in the reality show *The Apprentice*. His famous 'You're fired' line became his trademark, and his ostentatious stone-heartedness was sold to viewers as the very essence of toughness and get-real-ness. What wasn't anticipated was that one day those viewers would become his voters, and would change world history. The split of truth that trickled down from big wars to simple lives returned to the highest level of politics, and altered it in the most unprecedented way.

Trump quickly found out that playing 'the president' was not very different from playing 'the boss'. In October 2017 he flamboyantly threw paper towels to

Puerto Rican hurricane victims whose homes had been destroyed, their country's infrastructure demolished. As Trump grinned and the crowd cheered, shame was a stray dog that had long since given up on looking for its owner. Politics had become a mockumentary in which the president of the United States cruised into other people's realities only as a celebrity tourist. But at least he was only throwing paper towels, and not chess sets ...

In December 2013 Emine Erdoğan, the first lady of Turkey, with a hint of disgust on her face, joined her husband in throwing gifts including chess sets to a zealous crowd. The people, mostly poor, did not really know what the president and the first lady were throwing at them, but they nevertheless tried to catch the gifts as if their lives depended on it. Soon the crowd became wild, and a corridor of security was formed, with bodyguards separating the powerful from the mass of the crazed poor. The first lady, desperate to get the throwing business done with, sped up her throws, with the result that some of the gifts now hit people on the head. Human dignity was squeezed, squashed and finally pulped, live on TV; like Trump's paper-towel-tossing spree, it was truly 'disturbing footage' that ought to have come with a warning for those still capable of feeling shame.

As the shamelessness of the detached gradually became the dominant culture, those who found it difficult to live in such a manufactured *zeitgeist*, surrounded by a dominant majority who deemed shame and mercy naïve, were now beginning to hesitate whenever they felt the urge to shout, 'Shame on you!' I know, because I was embarrassed to be ashamed too.

'I guess I'm … mmm … ashamed. But then, maybe I shouldn't be, right?'
Here I am, in Paris in my expensive new blue raincoat, bought in honour of Leonard Cohen's song but with *petit bourgeois* uneasiness from a boutique in Saint-Germain. It is November 2006, and I'm creating a Mexican wave of irritation as I squeeze past the knees of the people seated in my row in the Odéon cinema. The film on the screen, Sacha Baron Cohen's mockumentary *Borat: Cultural Learnings of America for Make Benefit Glorious Nation of Kazakhstan*, ridicules both the Kazakh people and Americans who took part in it without being aware of its nature. Mr Cohen, playing his alter-ego the Kazakh journalist Borat Sagdiyev, is singing the so-called Kazakh national anthem, a made-up song which includes such boasts as 'Kazakh's prostitutes, cleanest in the region'. I must have given an exaggerated sigh as I stepped out of the cinema, because the ticket guy asks, 'Are you OK, madam?' I light a reviving cigarette and take the question too seriously: 'I guess I'm … mmm … ashamed.' The audience is still laughing inside, so

I don't stop there. 'But then, maybe I shouldn't be, right?'

A few days later, wearing my new raincoat while idly scanning the news over a morning coffee in a Parisian café, I suddenly lose my sense of chic as I read a piece by Patrick Barkham in the *Guardian*. It mentions the *Borat* movie, and the fact that Americans tend to sue when they are offended, as opposed to the Kazakhs, who are obliged to laugh along with their tormentor. The piece asks: 'Can there be a happy ending for those who feel ridiculed or exploited?'

I pause at the end of that sentence and remember a very old coat of mine, one I wore in the nineties. And a long-forgotten moment flashes before me, a moment in time when I was not only a picture-postcard of cool, but actually cool.

'You know the Russian whore I slept with last night? She turned out to be a cosmonaut!'

It is 1993, and Turkey isn't yet a small *land of plenty*. The choices are obvious for the young; we are reading newly translated Charles Bukowski and watching the Jim Morrison biopic. We are reading both Karl Marx and Francis Fukuyama's *The End of History*. The USSR has collapsed, and neoliberalism's yuppie heroes with their inexhaustible *positive energy* make leftists look like pathological pessimists, if not eternally defeated dreamers. Antagonism is *passé* thanks to the newly acquired decorum of identity politics, so we are taming our way of speaking, beginning sentences with 'I believe' and 'I feel', so as to shelter our political and moral convictions within fashionable mannerisms in the universe of multiple realities. In the new unipolar world we are reduced by triangulation to being 'well-meaning'. However, we are not clear what that means. Our political stances and moral frameworks float like a waterlily detached from its root, during a period when the grand texts of the Enlightenment are being trashed by the new stars of Western philosophy. We know better than to choose religion as the North Star of our hearts *in a heartless world*, but we are still too new to the world to imagine a secular morality. Besides, religion and theology are already being exploited as a political commodity by young radical Islamists. But, despite these political and philosophical inconveniences, we are discovering that even the crumbs of the previous century's political convictions might still be enough to keep our spines straight.

This is my second year at law school, and my first year as a reporter in Ankara. I am still trying to get my bearings in this landlocked capital. And whenever I feel disoriented in this fast-changing world, my armour and shield are my mother's long scarf, which she wrapped around herself in prison as a leftist student after the 1971 military coup, and my father's old coat, which he wore as a young lawyer when he got her released, and asked for her hand the minute she stepped out of her prison cell. The coat had big enough pockets to fit in Gramsci, William Blake, a packet of Camel Shorts and a Walkman that played Janis Joplin on repeat: 'Tryyyyy just a little bit harder!' Many kids of my generation have coats like this that date back to the seventies. They keep us warm, blanketing our confusion with the convictions of the previous generation.

One morning, at the entrance to university, before Janis has a chance to start screaming in my ears again, I hear the then popular joke: 'You know the Russian whore ...'

The joke is directed at a couple of broken-looking new students from former Soviet Turkic republics, Turkmenistan, or Kyrgyzstan, or maybe Kazakhstan. This is the first year Turkey has welcomed them as the orphans of a collapsed regime, and only because of their ethnicity, which they probably discovered after the collapse. Everybody can pick out this disoriented new species in the city, wandering in groups with their Iron Curtain two-piece suits and matching slip-on shoes of the centrally planned economy. They are real-life Borats, as it were. As if losing a country and all of a sudden ending up in the 'free world' is not enough, everyone is talking about their defeated system, but almost never to *them*. And now at the law school entrance they have to hear the dirty joke about their former fellow citizens. I stop and shout at the joker, 'Shame on you!'

It is a reflex reaction, an uncalculated act of expelling my vicarious shame at being a witness to this embarrassing scene, and returning the shame to its rightful owner. I have a responsibility to do so, for I happen to inhabit the same reality as them. Even my hesitant moral compass is clear on this one. And there are millions of kids like me, who would do the exact same thing had they heard the dirty joke. How clueless we all were of the fact that the coolest thing about us was that we still clung to a single, stubborn truth, an intact moral code.

Thirteen years later, as I put down my copy of the *Guardian* in the Parisian café, the feeling of shame, and the responsibility of returning it to its rightful owner when people are humiliated, is no longer a reflex; it comes with hesitation. *Maybe I shouldn't be, right?* As a self-loathing *petite bourgeoise*, I blame my famous blue raincoat, and miss the big pockets of the older one, which I could use to hide my hands when they felt too weak to change things. But I still cannot predict, as our mothers couldn't have anticipated the warnings of 'disturbing images', a world where the humiliated greets the perpetrator as his saviour.

'I salute Borat!'
On 23 April 2012, six years after the release of *Borat*, Kazakhstan's foreign minister Yerzhan Kazykhanov was

praising Sacha Baron Cohen in a speech in Parliament. The nation officially thanked the comedian that day because 'since the release of the film, visas issued by Kazakhstan have increased tenfold'. Some Kazakhs may have felt ridiculed and humiliated, but that wasn't too high a price to pay, considering the new flow of tourists. The Kazakh people were no longer upset; rather they celebrated having been, in Kazykhanov's words, 'put on the map' – the new map where people are perfectly content to have their island of reality visited by citizens of other islands only to be ridiculed, so long as they pay for it. They were no different from reality show stars who are happy to be confined in a constantly monitored house, or to starve on an island, as long as they are recognised as 'someone' in popular culture. To answer the question about *Borat* in the *Guardian* piece, there actually was a happy ending for those who were ridiculed and exploited, provided they were happy to be joining the global capital's world map of morality, where the losers – as in Donald Trump's *The Apprentice* or in the war-torn countries quickly reframed as tourist destinations – were fully content.

Since our moral compasses, which we assume to be less scrambled than the right-wing populists', no longer direct us to react as promptly as they did in the last century, perhaps we should just *try a little bit harder* to enjoy the shamelessness in this post-truth world. Meanwhile we can always busy ourselves by focusing on external manifestations of the problem: internet trolls, useful idiots, ruthless leaders, fake news and all the rest, again forgetting that even these are the natural consequences of the last decades.

It was in the 1980s that mainstream Turkish journalists started to feel comfortable inside the new moral framework; their right to unionise might have been stolen, but as compensation they were welcomed into sterile media plazas where they didn't have to dirty their newly imported Italian loafers. Dressed like corporate employees, they started calling their newspapers and TV channels 'the firm', and new supplements with English titles like 'Life Style' began appearing in their publications.

Around the time that Turkish journalists started not only reporting on, but also pretending to be the role models of, the new *bon viveurs*, Western journalism was beginning to obsess about the concept of 'objectivity'. It would soon be exported to the rest of the world, where journalists were becoming no longer street kids seduced by adventure, or vagabonds enchanted by the idea of finding the truth, but obedient corporate workers. This new type of objectivity was not conventional double-checking and be-fair-to-all-sides-of-the-story, rather it was the imposition of sterility. What was being called objectivity was really neutrality, with journalists holding the victim or the weak to the same level of interrogation to which they held the perpetrator or the powerful. Not surprisingly, this balancing act, this so-called objectivity, worked in favour of the powerful, the ones who talked about *realpolitik*, the weaponry. The space reserved for the 'naïve' on the split screens got smaller and smaller. Most mainstream journalists fell into line, consoling themselves with the fact that at least they were still presenting facts, not lies. In the new environment of ideologically transformed politics they mutated into smooth operators able to wander between the islands of realities while planting their flag of morality firmly on the conformist one.

By the 2000s, the essential moral grounding of journalism, as being the voice of the voiceless and questioning the powerful, was degraded to being the 'personal opinion' of the journalist. You were obliged to state in your social media profiles that whatever you wrote there was your 'personal truth', in order not to contaminate the neutrality of *the firm*. As a result journalists have been unable to prevent themselves from becoming the whipping boys of right-wing populist leaders whenever those leaders needed to demonstrate that they had a direct line to the *real people*. Thus the astonished journalists trying to hide their weakness behind giggles at the Trump–Putin G20 photo op in July 2017, when both leaders took direct aim at them.

* * *

110

In the last few years, especially since Donald Trump came
to power, it has become popular to reduce the problem of
post-truth to a contest between 'the mainstream media'
and social media trolls. Turning this giant political
issue into a boxing match between heroic Rocky and
ruthless Drago is convenient. The juxtaposition of
journalism versus post-truth both simplifies the matter
and distracts from the political history of post-truth and
the moral issue at its heart. Besides, at times it has been
beneficial for the established media to ignore the darker
complexity of the issue. As Trump put it crudely, the
New York Times's circulation soared both online and in
print as soon as the competing forces of fake news and
post-truth appeared on the political scene.

The big news networks also benefited from this political and ethical crisis by polishing up their tarnished
image as plucky fighters for truth against the dark
forces of politics. Trump himself said on 23 February
2018, in a speech at CPAC (the Conservative Political
Action Conference), that 'Even the media, the media will
absolutely support me, sometime prior to the election.
All those horrible people back there, they're going to
support me. You know why? Because if somebody else
won, their ratings would go down, they all would be
out of business. Nobody would watch. They all would
be out of business.' The transformation of newspapers
and news channels into corporations, which made
them addicts of profit (and therefore ratings and online

clicks), and thus eventually left less space for boring truths and facts, couldn't have been demonstrated more bluntly. It was as if Trump were reminding the press of the old journalistic adage: 'Follow the money.'

The Russian and Turkish governments have the same payment policy for their troll armies. The forces of the anti-science and anti-facts invasion are, ironically, paid roughly the equivalent of an associate professor's salary. Basically, if you are smart enough to fluff up the ideas on a list handed to you by your post-truth supervisor every day, to embellish them with some ruthless adolescent jokes and attack real people while hiding behind multiple pseudonyms, you are qualified for the job. Besides, for those who were born into this time of separate islands of reality, and who grew up armoured and shielded with cynicism, their job might be less of an ethical challenge and more of a behavioural survival method in our jungle of multiple 'truths'. They could even be considered good students of our age, bearing in mind the fact that what they've witnessed in their brief lives is that cruising between the islands, and mocking or trashing them, can earn you a good life – if not necessarily as wealthy as Paris Hilton's – or maybe even the American presidency.

After all, the job of a troll is relatively mundane. Their mission is not to discuss a topic or refute an argument, but to terrorise the communication space with unprecedented hostility and aggression, in order to force opposing ideas into retreat. Trolls are the digital pit bulls trained to bully away proper communication etiquette, rationality and substance from the social media sphere, while becoming the salaried role models of shameless cruelty for other social media users, the 'normal people' who then voluntarily enlist in the militias of immorality.

'People are incredibly cruel.'

In December 2016, many people must have thought this when eighteen-year-old Texan girl Brandy Vela shot herself in the chest in front of her parents following years of vicious cyber attacks. Perhaps the most incredible part of the story was that the bullying went on after her death, and her suicide became a source of mockery on social media for several days. Her father told interviewers that the police had told the family that they couldn't do anything about it.

The law does not only regulate our actual lives, it also sets the bar in terms of ethical minimums in human interaction. When people enter a lawless space, their interactions are left at the mercy of individuals or groups who have, throughout human history, taken advantage of such conditions. The digital sphere, which now informs the real-life political sphere, is still lacking in laws and law enforcement. Therefore, trolls and those inspired by their ruthlessness are cruel simply because they can be. Online, the extent to which they can exploit freedom of speech is limited only by their own moral codes – which, as we have seen, have been shaped to fit the dominant moral framework of recent decades. Therefore it is only natural that the 'How can they be so cruel?' question becomes the 'Where do all these cruel people come from?' question, as the voices multiply. That's when bewilderment turns into terror, a feeling of being surrounded by armies of the ruthless. In this age of post-truth, when mercy and shame are not sheltered by a political identity that enables people to act together on them, if your moral values are not politically organised, you can end up feeling quite alone.

Ali Ismail Korkmaz was nineteen when he died in a coma thirty-eight days after being brutally beaten by police officers and government-supporting shopkeepers during the Gezi protests in Turkey in the summer of 2013. His murder became the symbol not only of the cruelty of the government, but of the contagious cruelty among its supporters – the ordinary people who participated in his murder included three bakers. Video footage of the incident, during which Korkmaz begged his attackers to stop, sent shock waves through the entire country – at least among those who didn't believe that he deserved to die just because he was a protester.

I was one of the many journalists and human rights defenders who followed the ridiculous judicial process that followed. For 'security reasons' the court was set up in an extremely small room in a deserted state building in a remote city in Anatolia. The space was so packed that Korkmaz's mother's knees were almost touching her son's murderers. As if all these intentional physical obstacles and emotional torture were not enough, everyone who showed up at court was openly filmed by the police – the camera was rubbed up against our noses. But the most excruciating part was watching social media become filled with posts from trolls ridiculing Korkmaz and his family. The level of cruelty would have left anyone with a basic human sense of morality paralysed with horror. We were confined on a *Lord of the Flies* island where only Jacks resided. Those who had read the book might have been asking themselves, 'Where are all the Ralphs?'

The Ralphs are spending their evenings doing unpaid citizen journalism, trying to combat the trolls on social media who mock the weak in keeping with the spirit of the dominant system, only to wake up in the morning to hear the latest outrageous statement made by their leader. And all the while they are attempting to avoid the barrage of alternative truths from ever more unexpected angles – from the rejection of the roundness of the earth to the belief that anyone who commits adultery should automatically be thrown into prison. It is this mechanism, the perpetual motion of the outrageous act and the bewildered response to it, caught in a vicious circle, that is seized on by the right-wing populist leaders and used to destabilise social and political life.

'What do you think about the ongoing criminalisation-of-adultery discussion in Turkey at the moment?'
The BBC's Turkey correspondent Mark Lowen asked me this question during his programme on BBC World News in March 2018. I giggled sarcastically, which sounds horrible on a radio show unless you're a Middle Eastern listener. 'Well,' I finally said, 'the government must be doing something really bad elsewhere.'

It was a time when Turkish troops were entering Afrin, in Syria, and the first coffins were coming back to Turkey. So Erdoğan, as he has done dozens if not hundreds of times before, made an outrageous statement about something completely irrelevant in order to fire up public debate and overshadow the disturbing footage of the dead soldiers. The criminalisation of adultery has been brought up by the government at least a dozen times over the last two decades, and each time something else was happening that had to be concealed by the white noise of shocking statements. If it wasn't adultery, it was the banning of abortion.

In terms of utilising the technique of the outrageous act and the bewildered reaction to distract society and destabilise the political debate, women's rights is always fertile ground. In March 2018, Angela Merkel all of a sudden found herself having to deal with a long-overlooked Nazi-era abortion law. The law said that doctors were forbidden from advertising abortion, but nobody had paid any attention to it until Merkel's conservative new coalition ally decided to make it into a moral issue in an attempt to weaken Merkel and destabilise the political sphere. The conservatives, of course, mobilised their supporters to amplify the matter, and before German women knew what was happening, the country was preoccupied by a problem that many had thought belonged to the middle of the last century.

While those who were sane enough to acknowledge the absurdity of the situation were kept exhaustingly busy organising their political reaction, the right-wing populists seized on the opportunity to attract support from reactionary voters. The question of abortion is certainly a more accessible one than complicated financial issues, and much more useful when it comes to destabilising the political debate to consume opponents' energy. The trick was straight out of the Erdoğan playbook: periodically say something outrageous about women's issues; let the audience be shocked; and keep the controversy going until whatever you're doing behind the white noise has been accomplished.

The influential populist Polish politician Jarosław Kaczyński prefers cats over women when he needs the white noise. 'Let us not be fooled,' wrote opposition

MP Michał Szczerba on Twitter on 24 November 2017, after Kaczyński was seen reading a book about cats during the parliamentary hearing that would change the law concerning supreme court judges, and give the government more power in appointing them. All day long what Polish people saw on social media was not the details of the new regulation, but jokes or disgusted comments about Kaczyński reading a cat book. Szczerba's call for the population not to be fooled was too weak an alarm, and it went mostly unnoticed as the white noise invaded public perception.

But in terms of creating outrageously deafening white noise, America's first lady Melania Trump can teach Kaczyński and his cats a lesson or two. In June 2018, when boarding a plane to visit a child detention centre on the Texas–Mexico border, Mrs Trump wore a jacket that put her on the trending topic list for days. The immigrant children who were separated from their parents and forced to appear in court on their own were at the top of the political agenda, and the president was under pressure over the massive negative reaction to this cruel policy. Many members of the American public were desperate to show that they cared about the children despite their president's policies. However, the first lady's unprecedentedly cheap ($39) coat had the dominant moral framework's motto scrawled on its back: 'I really don't care. Do U?'

I imagine the reader of this book might have wanted to answer Mrs Trump's question by shouting back, 'Yes, I do care!' But then, how many of us can articulate the reasons why we care in clear sentences, without the use of prosthetic clauses like *I feel* or *I believe*? It is not just that what we have to say is drowned out by the white noise and the battering rams of right-wing populist politics. It is that there is no longer the certainty of a shared value system that would allow us to prove, with certainty, that a moral crime has been committed.

At the heart of our moral hesitations lies the fact that during the eighties the giant philosophical question of how to be a good person was frogmarched into the realms of religion and individual conscience. And thanks to largely uncontested neoliberal conservative mainstream politics, family became the only bastion in which the individual's need for brotherhood and solidarity was supposed to be fulfilled (except perhaps in the TV show *Friends*, where the characters encountered almost nothing that might test the strength of their solidarity). As morality was corralled into the holding pen of religion, religion itself was clipped and cropped into market-friendly 'spiritualities'. So on any given weekday you could start your morning with a meditation to help you rise above the material world and enjoy the lightness of being, or you could listen to a TV preacher's sermon on the importance of sharing, right before you started your daily quest for the *real* holy grail: profit. And thanks to the recently split screens of the human soul, this kind of moral patchwork is now individually tailored to fit each of our spiritual preferences.

When morality is exiled from public life and isolated in the private space of the individual, to be enjoyed only at certain times in our day, how can we know with any certainty that shame and mercy are shared concepts? And how can we convince people not to commit evil in those realms of public life from which law enforcement is absent? These are questions that can only be answered with the help of a secular morality, and while that may not yet have disappeared entirely, since the eighties it has gradually become more difficult for us to imagine. This is why over the last decades, whenever the voices of morality have tried to be heard, even those who were determined to shout their moral concerns have been forced to lower their voices and to ask the question, '*Maybe I shouldn't, right?*'

Truth is not a mathematical concept that needs to be proved with equations. Its singleness demands an intact moral compass, with certainties about what is good and bad. And that kind of certainty, dear reader, requires first a political perspective and then a political movement strong enough to fight not only the kings but also the gods. For standing in the way of such a political movement are not only the guardians of the thrones, but also, and more importantly, the normalised, and therefore invisible, assumption that humans cannot have moral convictions unless they believe in a god.

Well, well ... I admit, when the god issue comes up, one tends to retreat to the old safe playground: the troll issue, Russian collusion in US elections, fake news and the creation of an intellectual industry built on elaborations around the concept of post-truth. The *real* truth is that time passes more easily when we busy ourselves playing in this sandpit, which has actually been built for us by the kings who want to go back to those times when they were the only ones allowed to shoot the deer.

FOUR

Dismantle Judicial and Political Mechanisms

QUESTION: 'If you were American, who would you vote for?'

ANSWER: 'Trump. I am horrified at him. I'm just thinking that Hillary is the true danger ... In every society there is a whole network of unwritten rules, how politics works, and how you build consensus. Trump disturbed this. And if Trump wins, both big parties, Republicans and Democrats, will have to return to basics, rethink themselves, and maybe some things can happen there. That's my desperate, very desperate hope, that if Trump wins ... Listen, America is still not a dictatorial state, he will not introduce fascism. But it will be a kind of big awakening. New political processes will be set in motion, will be triggered.'

* * *

Appearing on Britain's Channel 4 News on 3 November 2016, just five days before the US presidential election, Slovenian philosopher Slavoj Žižek, rock star of modern-day Marxism, thought he could surprise his followers with the above statement. However, in Turkey his words were met with an exhausted shrug. Similar *desperate, very desperate* hopes had been expressed by Turkish political theorists before every election and referendum since Erdoğan first came to power in 2002. By the time Žižek came up with the idea, the notion that 'When the establishment is disturbed, a new political motion will emerge to better the politics' had become a tired cliché. Such a viewpoint has long been despised by dissident voices in Turkey, where those expressing these never-ending *maybes* have generally been seen as collaborators with the authoritarian regime the country has ended up with. When some of these cynical intellectuals became self-exiled in European countries, they made statements and gave interviews about how *Erdoğan suddenly turned out to be authoritarian*, and how *surprised* they were. Those who had resisted, who still lived under an authoritarian regime and were there on the front line fighting for democracy, defending its last stronghold, the ballot box, could only read about the way the exiles were *deceived*, and their *unpredictable* heartbreak, with scorn.

* * *

'*So here I am, gone from post-structuralist anarchist to ballot-box monitor! Yes,* everybody knows their place now!'

On 1 November 2015, this tweet became an instant classic in the ever-expanding repertoire of Turkish gallows humour. It was posted on the day of the general election, and was shared among the broad community of well-educated people who had volunteered for ballot-box monitoring. The countrywide web of volunteers was professionally organised thanks to the immense work and energy of those who'd joined the Gezi uprising in 2013, and had resolved to remain active in politics after the protests. The tragic essence of the joke, the fall from the heights of leftist theory to the hard cement ground of basic democratic practice, resonated with many. These were people who had preferred to remain on the theoretical side of things rather than engage with the *banality* of party politics, until one day they found themselves faced with the obligation to stop the Turkish government from committing yet another electoral fraud. Their intellectual capacity had been made redundant by the infantilised and pathetic state of the political climate, and they were reduced to standing at voting stations to ensure that ballot boxes weren't meddled with by Erdoğan supporters, as they had been in previous elections. Those who repeated the joke were also making reference to the preceding years, during which they'd watched with amusement as the establishment and its rotten state apparatus had been shaken and literally *deconstructed* by the ruthless spin doctors of a populist movement. The irony was that, previously, many of them had viewed modern democracy as mere window dressing for the neoliberal system, and had enjoyed seeing the state apparatus being punished for its hypocrisy. But now they were experiencing a strange about-turn, for they had to defend the political machine and protect a system of representative democracy that most of them found *passé*.

Unfortunately, long before election monitoring became an undeniable duty and turned many into 'militant citizens', a decade of right-wing populist rule had passed in Turkey, and had proved that the political universe did not follow the rules of nature laid out in Žižek's *great expectations*. Right-wing attacks on the establishment had certainly not created a *big awakening*. Nor had the damaged political structures (the state apparatus; the entire political machine, including the non-governmental organisations; or the very fabric of the country, subjected to years of political and moral beating) picked themselves up from rock bottom and reformed themselves – for two simple reasons. Firstly, unlike a physical space, the political universe had no resistant surface that one might call a 'bottom'; and secondly, even if you believed that politics had reached its nadir, there was no reason why it wouldn't stay there. However, this desperately hopeful cynicism continued to be influential, causing dissident voices to remain quiet during the sinking period, and for their owners to find themselves in a sort of limbo. The advocates of *great expectations* legitimised the deteriorating situation by reassuring the masses that they hadn't yet hit the bottom that would enable them to bounce back to the surface. Human nature has a tendency to believe hopeful statements even when reality keeps refuting them, and so the dissidents continued to wait for these *maybes* to come true.

In the end, this lingering sense of desperate hope not only caused a belated, and therefore ineffectual, political reaction, but also ruined people's faith in political theory, stripping opinion writers of their weight and credibility in the political sphere. And the others who had predicted the dark future could hardly resist the temptation to use 'I-told-you-so's when they spoke.

Speaking of weight, it seems necessary to point out the decades of intellectual weight-loss that the global left had been through during the 1980s and 90s. Leaving aside the details of the historical and economic reasons for the phenomenon, one should not forget the time when mainstream leftist opinion-makers enjoyed and savoured the comforts of reducing the left to producing cultural criticism while knowingly or unknowingly cutting our ties with the toils of the commoners, the *real people* of today. Since I was on board that same *Titanic*, I can confidently say that dissecting the *images* or deconstructing the *discours* with a lot of Theodor Adorno and Roland Barthes references was the violin concerto almost all of us most enjoyed then. We felt too smart to be sidelined by *realpolitik*, and our intellectual refuge was not only safe but also ethically *sort of OK*. Until of course our words started looking like useless embellishments on a global political wreck.

When people like our post-structuralist anarchist found themselves becoming the footsoldiers of democracy, monitoring the voting and counting process, they immediately smelled something fishy. Or rather, something oniony. It was a strong and horrible smell, one they may have felt they couldn't bear, but had to. By the end of this chapter, and hopefully before your own country has to endure a similar stink, you'll understand why the smell of onions is such an integral part of democracy. If you cannot tolerate their smell, then you may be in danger of losing the lesser of two evils – the imperfect democracy-establishment-state triumvirate – to an authoritarian regime.

When Recep Tayyip Erdoğan first hit the political stage, those who followed party politics from a safe and theoretical distance experienced a cynical sort of delight. Not unlike that felt by their peers in Hungary, Britain and the US when their own populists began to emerge. Erdoğan's AKP was constantly rattling the establishment with hit-and-run shock tactics: attacking prominent state figures previously thought to be untouchable, dismissing the consensus view, making passing mentions of withdrawing from international agreements. It sent an invigorating jolt through the political system, and was a wake-up call to politicians of all sides. On every TV channel, AKP spin doctors left distinguished establishment figures speechless with their audacious dismissal of political conventions, the sense of astonishment they caused only broadening their defiant populist grins. The tactic was simple: make an explosive statement during the debate, spread confusion or start a fight between the established centre-right and centre-left politicians, poke away at the country's fragile compromises, and wallow in the disarray before ending the debate by stating that neither side was in touch with the demands of *real people*, and that the demands of the street had long become disconnected from the establishment's political perception.

While this cabaret muddied political debate, certain cynical leftists sat glued to their TV screens, enjoying the spectacle of small-time, provincial men taking down the long-respected, if not feared, establishment. 'The periphery is finally grasping power in the centre,' was a fashionable analysis at the time, as it would be in the US after a year of the Trump administration, or in post-Brexit-referendum Britain. There was, of course, a hint of jealousy in this: the left had expected to be performing this *revolutionary* act themselves. Many of them were so enamoured of the political destruction that it took them several years to ask the crucial question: 'What are you going to replace the establishment with?' And when they finally remembered to ask the question, the years wasted on political voyeurism were gone with the wind, leaving them to face the real consequences of their *desperate expectations*. Remember those social media comments from young, educated people in post-referendum Britain that boiled down to 'I didn't know that this voting would be taken seriously.' When the new-generation *flâneurs* of politics realised that their votes were more consequential than Facebook likes, their new non-European lives were already being shaped by real-life politics, as our lives in Turkey have been shaped by the value-set of provincial conservative men.

Žižek was almost two decades late to the debate with his belief that an anti-democratic political organism might somehow prompt the building of a better democracy. But in Turkey the question had soon been answered with authoritarian practices, and when the new 'militant citizens' working in the field came face to face with the leader's zealous supporters, it became clear that it would be almost impossible to change their convictions, or channel their frustrations into creating a better democracy. The leftist cynics also learned that good manners and restraint are not enough to avoid a fistfight – sometimes a literal one – when confronted with the anything-goes thugs of an authoritarian leader.

During the 2015 elections in Turkey, our post-structuralist anarchist/militant citizen and all those who theorised and believed that there is a political bottom to hit had to physically grapple with government supporters trying to put fake votes in the ballot box. They had thought that this was the lowest life could sink to, until they experienced the referendum of 2017, on extending the government's powers following the failed coup. Once again volunteering to monitor ballot boxes, they soon drew the depressing conclusion that election fraud was even more brazen than the previous time. Although volunteers meticulously monitored the voting process, when the counting began and it became clear that Erdoğan would not win, the Higher Electoral Board changed the election law from one hour to the next, following pressure from the leader himself, and egregious fake votes for Erdoğan were deemed valid.

The opposition came to understand that, with the authoritarian regime having seized state powers, even if there were to be a political reawakening, it was almost impossible to stop the political tide with their accustomed political behaviour. They were hurtling down past the new political and moral bottom, unimaginable until it had actually happened. And as for our post-structuralist anarchist, like half the country who voted against Erdoğan in the referendum that made him sole ruler of Turkey, he felt this latest blow would be the death of him. He was not to know that the afterlife would be even worse.

The death of our particular anarchist, like that of Dario Fo's, wasn't at all accidental. It would have been foreseen much earlier had the progressive opinion leaders of the time not wasted years expecting a political metamorphosis to occur out of the total collapse of politics, and thus been quicker to inform the masses. As for the afterlife of our anarchist and his peers, in 2018, having gone through several nadirs, they had to listen to Erdoğan giving speeches three times in one day in which he called people like them 'marauders'. They were also explicitly threatened by the president, who said, 'If those who live in Cihangir or Nisantasi [the Soho and the Greenwich Village of Istanbul] are well-behaved, we won't touch them.' They were now expected to remain silent while burning in the hell of authoritarianism. And although when snap elections were held in 2018 they once again struggled to their feet to retake their places monitoring the ballot boxes, it was only to learn once again the lesson that they had already been taught by the 2017 referendum. So, many of them went back to *knowing their place*.

However, Žižek was right about one thing. When right-wing populism seizes power and intrudes upon the state apparatus, it triggers a strange kind of politicisation. Unfortunately, this is of a sort we can call panic politics; an inadequate defence against populism and its new political lows, and nothing like the 'awakening' Žižek might hope for. It is more like a fight between siblings in which the weaker one ends up lying on the sofa kicking out with his legs in an attempt to fend off the stronger one. And the swiftness with which the authoritarian leader acts, as he doesn't bother to observe *obstructive* legal regulations, leaves no time for the opposition to get back to basics or rethink themselves. The only option left is to keep kicking out for as long as their legs will last.

'Three strategies can be identified in response to the [German right-wing populist party] AfD's provocations. First, the emotional response: Cem Özdemir, the leader of the Green Party, recently gave a passionate speech on the floor, calling the party "racist". The video went viral. Second, pointing out the AfD's inconsistencies wherever it makes mistakes. Third, tackling false allegations with facts …'

Der Tagesspiegel editor Anna Sauerbrey, in an article for the *New York Times* on 14 March 2018, wrote about Germany's attempts to deal with its new right-wing populist main opposition in the Bundestag. She concluded by saying that none of the tactics had proved successful so far.

One might have expected more effective methods for the containment of populists from German politicians, for obvious historical reasons. But things are getting pretty desperate when even the Germans, who have produced the most important intellectual and academic literature on the subject, are no better at dealing with populism and its attempts to dismantle political mechanisms than my mother.

'There go the worried secular aunties! Ha ha ha!'

My mother, like many other secular and progressive middle-aged, middle-class Turkish women, was like a coal-mine canary in the early years of the AKP. While some public intellectuals were still waiting for something magical to happen, she was already certain that no political response would work unless the opposition deliberately mobilised the masses through grassroots networks. She was actually fulfilling Žižek's prediction of people starting to *rethink themselves and return to the basics of politics*. Many Turkish women like her had been political in their university years, so they more or less knew how to organise and mobilise people politically. However, the 1971 and 1980 military coups had cut off the moral and political ties between the educated middle class and the working class and underclass (something that also happened in Western countries, though by different means). It had been a long time since these women had come face to face with *real people*. In order to enact real politics, therefore, the most convenient tool at their disposal was the main opposition party – which was, of course, part of the establishment. Thus they found themselves in 2007 in what was, for many, the uncomfortable position of standing shoulder to shoulder with the 'corrupt' establishment and against the political choices of *real people*, at a time when – just as Hillary Clinton did to Žižek and several other political analysts – the establishment seemed the real danger.

Ironically, these women were mocked by the right-wing populist government and those enjoying the show through the prism of political theory with the same form of condescension. The label attached to them by both was 'the worried secular aunties', a put-down that referred to their so-called *detachment from the real people*. They ignored the unfair teasing and got to work. They started visiting poor, mainly government-supporting districts, knocking on every door to talk about the hypocrisy of the government. They gave speeches in coffee shops about rising conservatism and how it was dismantling Turkish society. However, all their political work ended up applying the same methods used by the coalition parties in the Bundestag: giving emotional speeches condemning the ruthlessness of the populists, calling out government policy for being inconsistent with party promises, and voicing hard facts against the government's sweet lies. They spoke about the need for a government to abide by the law, the need for equality, and how social rights are connected to the health of a democracy. They were careful, like their peers in Western countries, to *empathise* with the leader's supporters.

However, after each speech, carefully crafted so as not to offend AKP voters, a truck full of pasta, coal and dried beans – part of the government's political fieldwork programme – would arrive, pull up outside the venue, and AKP members would start handing out free food and other supplies to the locals, most of them women who'd come to listen to *the worried secular aunties*. Standing there like characters from a Virginia Woolf novel who'd accidentally stumbled into *Germinal*, my mother and the other ladies doubtless resembled Bundestag politicians, at a loss to explain how all their political experience and theory evaporated before the AfD politicians' crude narrative. If they'd been asked, *the worried secular aunties* of Turkey could have told the members of the Bundestag that they would have to come up with a fourth tactic, because right-wing populist politics is immune to the other three remedies. Furthermore, from their many years' experience, they could also have told Western societies – which tend to think their foundations are stronger than Turkey's, and better able to resist right-wing populism – that the final takeover does not happen with one spectacular Reichstag conflagration, but is instead an excruciating, years-long process of many scattered, seemingly insignificant little fires that smoulder without flames.

They could also have given a long lecture on the new type of right-wing crusade that reduces democracy to the ballot box, and how this subjugates political choices to fears of hunger, unemployment and, ultimately, social insecurity. And when democracy shrinks to being no more than a voting process, then the destiny of a country becomes inseparable from its single ruler's political existence.

'What can we do? We are hungry. Once it was the leftists, and now it's Erdoğan.'

In March 2007, four months before Erdoğan won his second general election, I was conducting interviews about poverty in the most forgotten parts of Istanbul. The people I spent days with were living on roadsides in tents and cardboard shelters, drinking water with worms in it, some of them dependent for heat on lumps of coal that their children collected from motorways, risking their lives and indeed sometimes dying in the process; it was a Charles Dickens universe without a storyteller, I remember thinking at the time. Many of them were AKP voters; they were the people who ravaged the free pasta and coal trucks that arrived after visits from *the secular aunties*. Talking to them, it became clear how Erdoğan himself not only controlled the main arteries of capital, but also how money travelled down capillary vessels to reach the poorest, building a complicated network of supporters whose very survival depended on Erdoğan's political existence.

In order to build such a giant web, Erdoğan's party exploited these people's already dire living conditions and, more importantly, gradually transformed their basic social rights into matters of party political charity. When people's needs are urgent, it's not hard to convince them that instead of fighting for social equality it makes more sense to show loyalty to a political party in return for a daily loaf of bread and a few lumps of coal. This charity was, of course, dependent on Erdoğan's generosity, which was only granted in return for votes.

In the beginning, the aid-in-kind distribution was concealed as religious charity, but later the party saw no reason to hide its preconditions for helping the poor, or its bias in distributing public services. By March 2018 it was no longer shocking to hear party spokespeople openly saying that new metro stations would be built according to political geography, and that AKP-voting districts would be given priority. This grandiose political operation, which ranged from distributing bread to supplying all kinds of public services, naturally required an incredible amount of micro-management, which Erdoğan and his party saw as being integral to their political crusade. Unfortunately, his political opponents' focus was on malpractice within the state apparatus and dealing with the aftershocks of populist politics in TV debates, whereas most of the hungry thought, 'As long as we're guaranteed bread, I don't care what the party is doing.'

As several people mentioned during my interviews, it had once been the leftist students who *expropriated* the bread and the coal and drove the trucks into the poor districts. Most of the poor couldn't really remember what happened to those young leftists, the country's political memory having been erased by the cruellest of military coups. It was too late, and also maybe ridiculous, to remind them that those students, in keeping with global changes in history, had turned into *secular aunties*. Besides, the aunties also had difficulty remembering those days, and how most of the time politics is based on bread and hope, not political concepts or depressing facts about malpractice within the state apparatus. It should have been the political theorists' job to remind people that unless there is social justice there is no democracy, but most of them were suffering from a forced amnesia that removed the term 'social justice' from the political lexicon. The secular aunties nevertheless could see that out on the streets the main question was both a simple and a crude one: 'Tell me why I shouldn't take the food when I am hungry?'

Meanwhile another web was being built, not around hunger but around unquenchable greed. This web involved the rich but powerless who found themselves queuing up before the ruler to get their share of wealth in the same hungry way as the poor. Although their story took place against the glamorous backdrop of palaces and five-star hotels, their neediness was exactly the same.

'Some have concluded that the problem is simply one of autocracy, that there is no longer any distinction between the Kremlin and Putin. As Vyacheslav Volodin, the current Duma speaker but then a high-level domestic policy aide to Putin, has publicly said, "While Putin is there, so is Russia; once Putin is gone, so is Russia." This conception of Putin as sole sovereign has developed only gradually.'

Gleb Pavlovsky, who served as an adviser to the Kremlin between 1996 and 2011, wrote the above in the May/June 2016 issue of *Foreign Affairs* magazine. A former spin doctor and one of the architects of Putin's Russia, Pavlovsky had waited until he'd fallen from grace to make his revelations about the evils of the regime. In his long article he explained how a plutocracy run by one man had been created in Russia by knitting together a vast web of vassals to act as a safety net for Putin's political power. By the time Pavlovsky's piece was published, it was too late to untangle this web that made Putin equivalent to the Russian state and the Russian people.

Ironically, only a few months earlier, on 16 March 2016, Erdoğan was giving one of his periodic speeches at the '*Mukhtars* Meeting', a political invention of his own in which he gathers three hundred or so previously insignificant, low-level neighbourhood authorities in his lavish palace to talk about whatever he wants to talk about, with a standing ovation guaranteed. As the *mukhtars* listened, for the most part oblivious to such topics as the American secretary of state's latest statement or Germany's recent change of policy on trade, the president suddenly said: 'They want me gone. When Erdoğan is gone, Turkey is destroyed.' He was not simply lavishing praise on himself, disguised as humility, as he frequently does, but was voicing what had generally come to be believed anyway, not only by his devoted supporters but also by many of his critics, who are suffering from a serious case of Stockholm Syndrome. Like Putin, from his early days in power Erdoğan created a loyal web of vassals, and gradually transformed the decision-making process for matters concerning the nation's finances until every economic transaction, from the most micro to the most macro, was in some way connected to him.

Needless to say, the first years of this process are always applauded by big finance, owing to the fact that the idea of a smaller state fits the dominant narrative of the neoliberal system. However, new right-wing populism's twist on the well-worn 'a smaller state is a better state' chorus is that through populist policies the leader becomes the single voice of wealth distribution and state power, in contrast to previous right-wing or liberal leaders who shared power with established big finance. And at times this single voice can be so arbitrary that even the leader's personal habits, likes or dislikes become preconditions for the wealthy to grab a bite from the cake of capital. For instance, one of Erdoğan's conditions for the rich was for them to stop smoking their big cigars and swallow some of their pride.

'... And so, my dear, some of the top ten richest people in Turkey were in that damned line queuing for omelette with their empty plates like a scene from Les Misérables.'

As soon as the established, secular financiers of Istanbul realised that the game had changed, and the only way to win giant public tenders and gain access to big bank loans was through the personal approval of Mr Erdoğan, their choice of action was not to rally the business world to protest or get politically organised to resist, but instead to do anything in their power to enter into the good graces of the leader. The most effective way to be accepted into his court was to 'get on the plane' – to be selected to travel abroad with Erdoğan in his presidential jet. All the owners of large companies, businesses that employed thousands, desperately tried to get rooms in the same hotels as Erdoğan, and some of them reluctantly had to quit smoking, because Erdoğan is very strict about cigarettes, never missing a chance to reprimand and embarrass smokers publicly. A financial reporter friend of mine couldn't help laughing when he told me of the farcical scenes that occurred on these trips, and how Erdoğan took immense pleasure in belittling or tricking these once-powerful people: 'You should have seen all these big bosses trying to hide their giant cigars whenever the elevator doors opened, and how they'd race to coincide with Erdoğan in the lobby, constantly using mouth sprays.'

All the fun of playing tag disappeared when the bosses of big finance realised too late that they were no longer required in Erdoğan's new Turkey, and that their businesses could be confiscated overnight if terror charges were laid against them. As a consequence, several major financiers moved their headquarters to London or New York. This was followed by a white-collar emigration, until Erdoğan, in 2018, started saying, 'If they want to go, we'll even buy their plane tickets for them.' By then he had built his own class of bourgeois supporters and money men, and they were all he needed to run his charade of democracy. The big companies that left Turkey were then labelled 'marauders', a term they themselves had long thought was only applied to leftists or post-structuralist anarchists. And many were dismissive of the fact that this process had begun years ago, with a seemingly insignificant phenomenon that occurred in remote provincial towns in Anatolia.

* * *

'*What about those prayer rugs on top of every office bookshelf?*'

Here I am, in 1997, in a godforsaken town in the middle of Anatolia, sitting with some small-time businessmen and some very young Istanbulite women in a music hall.

'Music hall' is a code name. Almost every pious little Anatolian town has one of these places. They are mostly out of town, on the highway, a way to keep sinning out of conservative provincial life: the prostitutes, the alcohol and all the other *dirty* things, such as wining and dining in a mixed crowd. And here I am, drinking with them because I am doing a long piece about the 'Anatolian Tigers', a baby version of the Asian Tigers of the era, emerging capitalists of the free-market economy. After spending several weeks touring the most conservative towns in Anatolia and talking to middle-ranking, pious businessmen, I had started asking myself existential questions. And somehow, in a state of stupor, it had seemed like a good idea to start drinking with a bunch of men who saw me, as a female journalist, in much the same way that they saw the Istanbulite prostitutes sitting at the same table. So the men loosen up, I loosen up, and thanks to courage acquired by some sense of unspoken solidarity with the prostitutes, the only women in the place except me, I ask the question that has been dogging me for days. '*What about those prayer rugs ...?*'

For several days, in every interview I've conducted in every ostentatious provincial office, I've come across the exact same thing: a bookshelf full of untouched *Encyclopaedia Britannicas*, probably a promotion from some newspaper, and on top of the bookshelf the cheapest kind of prayer rug, *the prayer rugs of real people* before *real people* were even a thing.

The men giggle, something they wouldn't have done in the city with a woman, and certainly not with a woman asking about prayer rugs, the holy fabric of every practising Muslim. One of them answers while the others offer approving grins and nods: 'If we don't put that rug up there, nobody will do business with us.'

Then they told me – amidst a lot of crude sexual jokes, of the kind repressed men tell when they meet an *open* woman (which unleashes the caged adolescent in them) – about how money travelled along politicised, religious sect lines, and how most people were really just pretending to be pious, in order to be able to move in the moneyed circles. This was years before the AKP was even established, but the new conservative, provincial *bourgeoisie* was already taking off. A few years after this interview, those new Anatolian businessmen became powerful enough to demand political representation, and the AKP was established with their support.

What I remember most from that music-hall night is that one of the men whispered a weird question to me: 'Do you really need a membership card to get into a disco in Istanbul?' He'd been turned away at the door of one, supposedly because of the card issue, and wanted to make sure the bouncers hadn't been lying to him. 'No,' I said, sorry to wound his small-town pride. 'There's no such thing as a membership card for discos.' Years later, that same businessman bought the disco to which he had been refused entry and turned it into a 'family restaurant', which in Turkey means a conservative no-alcohol establishment. After Erdoğan came to power, all those men, and dozens of their ilk, gradually moved to Istanbul to take over the businesses that secular businessmen had had to leave behind, largely due to Erdoğan's political and legal pressure.

This giant web that connected big finance and daily bread to political grants – such as unsecured loans from state banks or selling state-owned institutions to his close circle of friends – formed the bedrock of Erdoğan's support, and enabled his devotees to transform the state apparatus until the state became synonymous with its leader. Eventually the idea that 'When Erdoğan is gone, Turkey is destroyed' was not just a myth manufactured by the propaganda machine, but a solid political reality that meant an entire lifeline would be cut if Erdoğan lost power. It was not, therefore, only out of political conviction that the party apparatchiks got into fistfights with the election-monitoring volunteers (including our post-structuralist anarchist). They really were fighting for their lives.

It's not hard to imagine what we might be capable of were our daily bread, our house, our job or our business at stake. And if you can't imagine, you can always ask the people of Siklosnagyfalu, a village in southern Hungary.

'In winter there really isn't much work to do. There are days when we don't do anything.'

Gyongyi Orgyan, a resident of Siklosnagyfalu, said this to a *New York Times* reporter on 3 April 2018, a few days before the general election in Hungary. She was one of the many who had benefited from the made-up jobs that right-wing Hungarian leader Viktor Orbán provided villagers with in order to build his safety net of voters. During the eight years of his second term as prime minister, by supplying the unemployed with menial state-paid seasonal summer jobs designated by local government which took only a few hours a day, Orbán had lowered the unemployment rate from 11.4 to 3.8 per cent. This provided him with thousands of loyal supporters whose daily bread depended on his re-election. His power base was the poor and those who benefited financially from his regime, who became, as Jan-Werner Müller called them in a *New York Review of Books* piece, 'the nouveau riche, a civic-minded, conservative bourgeois'.

Although Müller called this 'Orbánomics', the same pattern is discernible in Erdoğan's regime and that of the novice populist leader Donald Trump. Only one day later, on 4 April 2018, the *New York Times* reported from northern Minnesota on a similar case of a network of grateful voters built upon seemingly outrageous economic decisions. On the front pages of the US papers, big business expressed alarm at Trump's tariffs on imports from China, but according to this rather overlooked story, the workers in Minnesota's taconite mines were delighted with the decision, and in fact Trump's 'madman tactics' for the economy were shifting the area's political geography from several decades of voting Democrat to voting Republican.

Weighing up such news, it's easy to reconsider the idea of building a wall between Mexico and the United States and see it as a long-awaited job opportunity, a glimmer of hope for thousands of construction workers. One might also ask how many *New York Times* readers would be prepared to give their own blood, sweat and tears to protect democratic institutions in a fight against the hungry masses. Or how many of Trump's critics would have the time and energy to transform themselves into militant citizens to stop the tide. More to the point, who among the big financiers would refuse to invest in such an enormous public construction project because of moral and political reservations? I can already picture thousands of construction workers gathering for a demonstration to shout, 'If the wall goes, America goes with it,' their free lunches, along with social media promotion, provided by the companies that won the tender. After Turkey's experience, I can even picture another thousand people at the rally who have nothing at all to do with actually building the wall, shouting their heads off just because they have been handed free hot dogs. This has been the case at hundreds of AKP rallies in Turkey, where our democracy may be less mature and the establishment weaker, but people starve in the exact same way.

So, what UKIP's Nigel Farage says in a Dorset pub, or what Trump supporters feel in Kentucky, is not really the issue when it comes to populist politics taking over the state. What matters most is whether Dorset pub-goers have accumulated the financial wherewithal to support the insanity or not. Or whether Trump supporters in some rural county far from the capital are actually building new economic networks that might look like a joke at the beginning, but end up being far from funny. The important questions at the heart of the real power of populism concern the reorganisation of financial transactions and economic relations: whether the new economic winners are numerous and established enough to require new political representation, and whether the economic networks they build are strong enough to create a safety net for the populist leader to seize the state powers. However, when one starts to witness the invasiveness of this wealth-or-bread-related political operation and how formidable it can be, one is forced to build mind shelters to protect one's sanity.

'Oh, they wouldn't let him do that.'

In living rooms across the United States, and any European country where right-wing populism is seizing state power, this abstract line is uttered by people watching the evening news whenever the populist leader does something formerly considered off-limits. From the Turkish experience, I know how annoying it is to hear the obvious question: 'Who is this *they* that will stop him doing whatever he wants?' In Turkey, the answer initially varied according to the political stance of the person being questioned: 'Well, the establishment'; 'The army of course'; 'There are elections coming up, the opposition will unite to stop this'; 'The deep state won't let this happen'; 'The people won't be deceived to such an extent.' But all these trusted, cast-iron fulcrums are eventually melted down and turned into swords by the populist leader, and the country is left to face the brutal power of the regime without the curbing, imaginary protection of any state institution or democratic practice. At least, that is what I said to the Obama Foundation CEO David Simas when I met him in Oxford on 11 April 2018, and it probably sounded too pessimistic to him at the time.

'These are mind shelters. For a year the American opposition trusted impeachment as a tool to stop Trump. After a year, when impeachment turned out to be a far-fetched legal and political option, they redesigned their mind shelter to talk about the mid-term elections.'

Simas, Obama's former political adviser, smiled politely at me when I said this during our Skoll World Forum panel discussion on 'Populism, Polarization and Civic Engagement'. This was right after he had mentioned his hopes that the coming mid-term elections would weaken Trump. He was, just as many of us had been in Turkey, concerned about the polarisation Trump had created, and about finding ways to overcome the tension it had produced. And his solution was no different from the one that many of us in Turkey had tried: to strengthen the social ties of citizens through empathy, and to create more sincere forms of communication between Trump lovers and haters. Although this approach was well-intentioned, I could see it resulting in thousands of Americans – like Turkish people before them – spending too much time trying to establish some form of connection with Trump voters, when the situation urgently required far deeper political solutions than a form of couples therapy – especially when their populist leader was making serious decisions at top speed, disturbing traditions previously considered unshakeable. Only seven months later Donald Trump, while claiming a dubious victory in the US mid-term elections, was ruthlessly attacking a CNN reporter at a White House press conference. His unheard-of tone and attitude were endlessly replayed on all the global news networks. CNN subsequently sued the White House for banning its correspondent only a year after it had sought to share emotional common ground with right-wing populism. And speaking of top speed, by the time you read this book you will probably realise that you have already forgotten some of the incidents it describes, which at the time seemed shocking, incredible and unforgettable.

Only three days after the Skoll World Forum panel, NATO's bombing of Syria changed the agenda again. Britain's prime minister Theresa May, France's prime minister Emmanuel Macron and the USA's President Trump, all facing domestic instability, joined together for the 'one-night-only' bombardment because of reports of a chemical weapons attack on civilians in the city of Douma. Vladimir Putin and the Syrian government argued that no such attack had been carried out, the Western powers didn't bother too much to try to convince the international community, and legendary British journalist Robert Fisk went to Douma and reported in the *Independent* that he found no evidence of a chemical attack. Leaving aside the dispute about whether the attack took place or not, there was neither parliamentary consent nor even a hasty international consensus for the bombing. The speed of events left no time for the opposition to *rethink themselves and return to the basics*, or to try to *empathise* with those who were clamouring for some sort of military response, for that matter.

One day before the bombardment, on 13 April, I was on stage at the Lincoln Center in New York sitting beside, of all people, the former secretary of state and Democratic presidential candidate Hillary Clinton. She was moderating the Women in the World Summit panel, 'The Gathering Threat: The Rise of Autocrats'. I was telling the three thousand or so guests about imaginary trust in state institutions and our illusions, our false belief that they can save democracy from the insanity of populist leaders. The decision to bomb Syria had already been taken, and the people of three countries, without having had a chance to give their approval of the military action, were once again being seen by many around the world as warmongers. Meanwhile, after this sudden political decision that had bypassed the checks and balances that were supposed to control them, Trump, May and Macron found themselves being hailed by their supporters as the true leaders of their nations. It struck me as remarkably reminiscent of the enthusiasm that is often shown to infamous populist leaders such as Putin and Erdoğan ...

The audience in the Lincoln Center could only applaud in desperate protest against being seen as members of a warmongering nation. In the following days Theresa May was questioned in Parliament about an act that had already been carried out. Her answer boiled down to: 'The operation was in our national interest. Assad used chemical weapons against his own people, and that is against international law, so we acted.' Full stop. The nation had to rally behind the leader, as it always does at a time of perceived crisis. With their unstable domestic politics, neither May nor Macron is likely often to be described as a populist leader *per se*, but the way they both danced through this international crisis more or less imitated the populist leaders' technique of swift moves with little need for public debate, and their perception of the ideal nation as a unified force behind its leader.

Just a few days later, in a similar fashion, Erdoğan announced an early election in the hope of consolidating his power once more, even though it went against all political precedent and despite the fact that the third largest party's leader was in prison on terror charges, along with thousands of other political prisoners. The election was 'in our national interest', naturally. As with the US, Britain and France, it was too late in Turkey to dampen Erdoğan's supporters' enthusiasm and tell them that the state and its legal system were being bypassed, and that this would set a new precedent for political practice whereby leaders could exercise their limitless power whenever and however they felt like it. The irony in this story is that throughout the three days I spent at the Skoll Forum and the Women in the World Summit I repeatedly heard people utter the same sentence: 'Oh, they wouldn't let him do that.'

For reasons I can't fathom, many remain blind to the fact that their leaders, wherever they sit on the political spectrum, are bothering less and less to ask for consent or approval. Over those same few days Trump was attacking the CIA and the FBI, replacing high-level officials in both organisations and rejecting the bipartisan FBI investigation into Russian collusion in his election campaign. It wasn't hard to picture a room somewhere in the dark corridors of the CIA headquarters, at the very heart of the American establishment, where agents were telling each other the same thing: 'They wouldn't let him ...' The habit of imagining our institutions as powerful, abstract beings, and forgetting that *they* are actually people who might be too paralysed to react, is a classic failure when grappling with authoritarianism, even for the executives of those very institutions.

The critical turning point in the long process of dismantling state apparatus and legal mechanisms is not the establishment of cadres made up of obedient and loyal party or family members, as many people tend to think.

The twist that enables leaders to play at will with this apparatus begins with them undermining it in order to create a sense of it being *superfluous*. In no time, the game-changing questions creep into public debate: 'Do we really need these institutions?'; 'Do we really need six top-level positions in the US State Department? Haven't they been vacant for over a year, and business has gone on without them?'; 'What is the British Parliament for if it is not needed even when deciding to commit an act of war?'

While creating this general sense of a superfluous state, through an energetic propaganda machine and the support of devoted masses who rely on the party's charity, the populist leader starts to strengthen the idea that his and his supporters' power is actually greater than that of the establishment. During the time that the establishment fails to respond or react to the leader's elbowing out of the legal process, a new general sentiment is born: 'It turns out,' people start to think, 'that what we considered to be a fundamental power was just a paper tiger all along.' Yes, even the CIA, the FBI and the Supreme Court! It's as if the leader, by constantly playing around with these institutions, is indirectly sending a message to the masses: 'You see, the palace of power is empty. Let's get in and take over.' What is important about the early attempts to disempower these institutions is not the actual changes, the new appointments or whether decisions such as bombing Syria are right or wrong, but rather the creation of a public sentiment that the state apparatus is doomed, and has long been awaiting a looting by the *real people*. After this, the next election becomes a formality, a simple matter of approving the leader's right to keep running the country and distributing the looted public wealth to his supporters. For in order to keep presenting the masses with the political bounty, the leader must also keep the election machine running unceasingly: elections mean reshuffling the pack and giving hope to new individuals or groups that they might now hit the jackpot and benefit from state wealth.

'Is there an upcoming local election, or something else that I don't know about?'

After making me translate numerous posters and billboards into English, my German journalist friend asked me if Turkey had entered another election cycle. The things were scattered about here and there on small overpasses, road-repair barriers, municipal construction sites. They all had pictures of Erdoğan kissing babies or cutting red ribbons, and were accompanied by 'Thank you's directed at him and his district mayors in Istanbul. 'There is no election,' I replied, 'but not a day goes by when we're not subjected to propaganda as if there's one in just a few days.'

The double game the populist leader plays is perfectly represented by these sycophantic messages put up by

AKP mayors. The unceasing election atmosphere they create allows the leader to play two roles at once. He becomes not only the state itself, but also acts as if an opposition leader is trying to snatch away state powers. Add in the manufactured political illusion of attacking the establishment while actually becoming the establishment, and it's easy to see why criticising a populist leader is like Bruce Lee attacking mirror images of the villain. When you criticise the leader as being in sole control of the state apparatus, he assumes the role of opposition leader, and when you try to catch him there, he jumps back into his role of being the state itself, reprimanding the opposition for being obsessed with party political disputes. The populist leader paralyses the political mechanism while gradually invading the state apparatus. Party and state become one; the leader needs state powers, yet they disintegrate whenever he needs to evade criticism. And meanwhile the state apparatus, the paper tiger, becomes smaller and smaller, until it becomes a paper ball to play football with in the lavish palace of Erdoğan, or golf at Trump's Mar-a-Lago.

The legal body that is imagined to be sitting on top of the body politic is certainly not immune to the populist leader's meddling. As long as the state is profitable, the leader can rely on a political climate in which fewer and fewer people question the dismantling of the legal system, and it becomes easier to label the ones who do so as terrorists. When victims of the oppressive regime who defend the rule of law are then arrested for making 'terrorist propaganda', their howls of protest fall on deaf ears. At this point, anyone who, in Erdoğan's words, 'obstructs the way' becomes a terrorist who must be locked up so as not to interrupt the smooth flow of business. It is no coincidence that, like Erdoğan, the Conservative government in Britain and the Trump administration in the United States view the rule of law as an obstruction to the will of the people whenever the judges – or 'the enemies of the people', as Britain's *Daily Mail* and the Turkish-government-supporting mainstream media call them – rule against the government. Thus the ignorance and partisanship mobilised by the populist leader can reach such a zenith that the *real people* of a country can end up becoming more dangerous than members of Al Qaeda.

'It's the only time in the whole of my judicial career that I've had to ask for the police to give us a measure of advice and protection in relation to the emotions that were being stirred up,' said Lord Chief Justice John Thomas in March 2017. As the most senior judge in England and Wales, Thomas's crime was to decide against the British government, ruling that it legally needed Parliament's assent before it could invoke Article 50 and begin the process of leaving the European Union. It was a decision that led to him receiving death threats from furious Brexiteers, who seemed more menacing than the Al Qaeda members he had previously ruled against. The journalist Nick Cohen was right when he wrote in the *Guardian* on 3 February 2018: 'In Russia, Hungary, Poland, the US and Venezuela, we have seen elected autocrats sweeping aside, or attempting to sweep aside, constraints on their power. They have the people's mandate. Anyone who stands in their way is therefore an enemy of democracy itself … Just because it hasn't happened here does not mean the British can console themselves with the happy thought that it can't happen here.'

The most alarming aspect of this process is that the time between such articles being written and laws actually being passed that criminalise any kind of criticism of the ruling party is far shorter than any American or British citizen, clutching on to centuries-old pillars of state, would like to believe. And when the court cases start being launched they seem bewildering at first, but swiftly become too numerous to stop, let alone to analyse.

'It must be more than 160 hearings in 2017. This is not the total number, of course. These are the ones I could attend. And some coincided with other hearings, so we had to split to attend as many as we could. The other day I guess other people were worried about the

start of a Third World War in the rest of the world, but I couldn't even read the news. We are being horribly beaten by these court cases, my friend.'

Elif Ilgaz is a former journalist, and now – like many without a job – she attends the political court cases in Turkey as an activist. She is one of the most prominent figures among the press community who did immense work for imprisoned journalists. She is laughing bitterly as she tries to calculate the number of court cases she had to attend during 2017: academics imprisoned because of peace petitions, students arrested for one thing or another, unionists, teachers, the list goes on. Her twins were in primary school when she started as an activist, and they are now taking their university exams. 'Our life is now lived between courtrooms, dear. We can do nothing else. Nothing,' she said to me on the phone a few days after the Syrian bombardment. This has been the life of the opposition in Turkey for years, their calendars filled with multiple daily hearings which not only leave them almost no time to organise any other kind of resistance, but also, as I will describe in the final chapter, make them feel humiliated and power-less, as if they were part of some giant cosmic joke at their own expense. I remember that it started with some of us writing articles like Nick Cohen's. But then, in no time, one very early morning in 2010, Ahmet Şık, a journalist and 'one of us', was taken by the police from his apartment and branded a 'terrorist'. As he was being pushed into the police car, he shouted, 'This is a mafia state! And it will come for whoever touches it!'

'[In his book Orbán: Hungary's Strongman*] Paul Lendvai is unsure how to classify Orbán's regime. In the end Lendvai settles on the term "Führer democracy" to emphasize the extraordinary centralization of power in Orbán's hands. And he endorses the idea of the "mafia state", a term coined by the Hungarian sociologist Balint Magyar to suggest that the reign of Fidesz [Orbán's political party] has little to do with political ideas, but is simply the means for a "political family" to plunder the country under the protection of its godfather.'*

This review by Jan-Werner Müller was published in the *New York Review of Books* in the first week of April 2018. It was only a month after Ahmet Şık was finally released from prison for the second time, after serving a sentence of more than a year. Paraded before the cameras, he couldn't stop himself from shouting again, 'This is a mafia state!' Thanks to the strict limitation on books in his high-security prison cell, Ahmet was probably unaware of the Hungarian sociologist who'd coined the term, but after being imprisoned twice, each time going several months without a hearing for his ridiculous terror charges, he knew from experience that *whoever touches the godfather will burn.*

* * *

161

After that first, shocking arrest, I wrote in my column: 'The time has come: they will now do the things you think they cannot.' I meant things about which many people thought, 'Oh, they'd never let Erdoğan do that.' The court cases that left hundreds of secular commentators, members of the army, journalists, political activists, unionists, academics and intellectuals – like Ahmet Şık – incarcerated did not come out of nowhere. For months, pro-government media had been using black propaganda to conduct character assassinations of these 'terrorists'. Government-supporting journalists targeted people, labelled them criminals and then openly called upon prosecutors to arrest them immediately. With the political climate sufficiently charged, it became dangerous for prosecutors not to arrest these public figures, for the prosecutors themselves would then become the targets of black propaganda, for not responding to the call of the *real people*, the party.

For a while, saying, 'Good to see you. So you haven't been arrested yet!' became a popular joke among journalists, academics and dissident figures in Turkey. Whenever one of us was targeted by the pro-government media and barraged with a mass of black propaganda, friends would call and say, 'Don't worry, we'll be publishing a newspaper together in Silivri soon.' Silivri was the huge, newly built, high-security prison that looked like a cement monument to the authoritarian regime. Located just outside Istanbul, it has its own

162

courtroom, to make it easier for the accused to come to court hearings before returning to their cells, and more difficult for their friends to attend and witness the farcical judicial process. Most of the hearings involved responding to black propaganda, with the onus always on the 'guilty' to prove themselves innocent, never the other way round. Since this was a *war against terror*, since there was a *national interest*, the judiciary no longer had to obey proper laws, but was free to follow the insane whims of those whose job it was to spread lies about anybody who did not bow before the godfather. I remember at one point, over the course of a single week, prominent figures producing no fewer than seven columns for the same pro-government newspaper calling for the prosecutor to arrest me. But I was one of the lucky few who despite being subjected to black propaganda saw the inside of Silivri prison only as a visitor, to see Ahmet Şık.

'Black propaganda in this country has never been so sophisticated and so effective.'

I'm at the Reform Club in London – one of the many institutions the British think can never be shaken because it has an impressive building with big old columns – drinking tea with the journalist Patrick Cockburn. We are talking about right-wing populists' black propaganda against opposing political figures. The *Sun*'s 'Jeremy Corbyn and the Commie Spy' story hasn't been published yet; that 'bit of James Bond' story, to use Corbyn's words, in which he was accused of selling state secrets to a Czech spy, would appear in February 2018. Still, the times in Britain were interesting enough to draw similarities with Turkey, although with caution.

Cockburn is more inclined than me to point out the differences as much as the parallels: 'Britain is the only country where the opposition offers a real option. It's not the strong establishment, but having this option might save the country.' He mentions Corbyn's nationalisation project, a vision that surpasses those of other social democratic parties in Europe and Turkey, where progressive oppositions have failed to come up with such a bold proposition on behalf of the poor against social injustice. Cockburn knows what I'm getting at, trying to see the similarities between the two countries and to build an argument that right-wing populism is a rising global movement that operates with the same pattern in every country, regardless of how robust its establishment or how mature its democracy. Indeed, it is the purpose of this book to draw attention to these patterns. But he is determined to stay relatively optimistic about the UK.

Eventually I ask him about the rising number of applications by British citizens for Irish passports after the Brexit referendum, and tell him the story of a friend.

'Here's the thing: this friend of mine, I mean, ideologically he's beyond nation states and he's never mentioned Ireland to me before, but he had an Irish grandma and so after the referendum he, like fifty thousand others, applied for an Irish passport to keep himself as a European Union citizen. And now he tells me he feels Irish all of a sudden, and he's hardly even been to Ireland. So do you think, years after the Good Friday Agreement ...'

Before I can finish, Cockburn cuts me off with an even more interesting story.

'A few years ago the Portuguese and Spanish governments said Sephardic Jews would be eligible for passports as an "act of atonement". You know, after the expulsion of tens of thousands of Sephardic Jews in the fifteenth century by crusading monarchs. Before Brexit nobody took it seriously. But now British Jews are trying to trace their family history back to the Middle Ages so they can apply for a second passport.'

We slowly move on to discuss the border situation in Northern Ireland, post-Brexit and how ethno-nationalist tensions might play out in British politics. Cockburn sees no reason for the tensions not to be activated again. 'This is what happens,' I say loudly, shattering the sombre atmosphere of the Reform Club. 'Right-wing populism pokes away at the country's fragile compromises until they become active tensions, in order to carry out its invasion of the state apparatus. Dismantling the judicial mechanism and paralysing the dissident masses through court cases is far easier when

the leader can call people terrorists, and when members
of society are too polarised to support each other in the
name of equality before the law. It's just like Turkey.'

Of course, most members of the British establishment would, upon hearing me compare Great Britain
to Turkey, call me 'passionate', the very worst thing
you can be in Britain, after 'interesting'. But Cockburn,
doubtless because he has seen first-hand how things
have panned out in Middle Eastern countries and
Turkey, knows where I am coming from. So we fall
silent, proper Reform Club silent.

As I walk out onto Pall Mall and towards Piccadilly
Circus, passing centuries-old buildings, members-only
clubs and lovely old arcades, I wonder how many of
the well-to-do people around me would be prepared to
defend the Good Friday Agreement if things got rough.
Or how many of them were willing to join the demonstrations to condemn the Syrian bombings as illegal,
especially when the British government's stated policy
was to create a 'hostile environment' for immigrants?
More importantly, how many British citizens would
choose to defend their social rights rather than collect
the crumbs falling from the high tables of the winners
of the system as political charity when they know that
they might die in a hospital corridor due to a paralysed
National Health Service? How many pillars would it
take to make democracy stand up straight in a country
where dozens of people burn to death in a low-income

tower block in London as a result of cost-cutting measures by the local council, as happened on 14 June 2017? When the opposition cannot be as nimble as the money, and when social injustice is ignored to devastating effect, that is when democracy starts to smell funny. Indeed, it begins to smell like rotting onions.

'No, you have to eat the onions. For democracy's sake, darling!'

Grigoris Bekos, my Greek editor, is quite a character, increasingly rare in the age of Facebook, when everyone looks the same but tries to seem different. It is a typically hot day in Athens in the summer of 2016, and we are launching two of my books that have been translated into Greek. I have six interviews lined up in a row, so Grigoris stations me on a hotel rooftop that overlooks the Acropolis. For each interview I pose in front of a backdrop of the birthplace of democracy, and I am speaking about democracy; it's impossible not to get the message.

During the interview marathon Grigoris kindly allows me ten minutes for lunch, and I am attacking a wonderful Greek salad as viciously as any Turk who's just spent several weeks in London, where the food tastes like a desperately ambitious experiment. But then I realise, 'Oh shit! It's got raw onions in it, I'll stink for the journalists.' Grigoris speaks, as always, in royal fashion: 'Darling, if you're defending democracy, you have to eat the onion and like the smell.' I laugh, but he continues: 'Did you know the citizens of Athens used to climb that mountain every day and go up to the Acropolis with a loaf of bread and an onion tucked under their arm? You see, they didn't want to starve up there while building the very first democracy. Democracy is a difficult job, darling, and it certainly doesn't smell of flowers.' He raises his finger as if marking history and says, 'Therefore onions are integral to democracy.'

I remember a friend of mine, Emre, the owner of a big textile company in Istanbul, coming back from ballot-box monitoring on the night of 1 November 2015 and saying, 'The AKP guys brought in this pitta, and my God, the room stank of onion for the entire day. As if struggling with them wasn't hard enough already.' Though onion is the one thing he cannot stomach, he remained right where he was until the ballot box was sealed. He had to stay there, in fact, to atone for all those past years when he thought he couldn't have stood the smell of onions, of practical politics, of real life. He laughed bitterly and referenced the famous post-structuralist anarchist's joke: 'As Erdoğan said, now *I know my place*! It is with the onion-eating people, apparently!'

FIVE

Design Your Own Citizen

She is not crying, and I am not holding her hand; that's not the way badass women enter an abortion clinic. I am carrying a chocolate cake, her sole wish for the 'after-party'. There was enough crying last night anyway, when she said, 'I can do everything on my own. I've *done* everything on my own in this fucking country. But not this. I cannot include a child in my war against misogyny.' By 11.30 p.m. she'd quietened down, decided to put the emotional *shit* on hold until her next therapy session.

So here we are at the clinic, looking like two hungover rock stars in our giant sunglasses. She is now putting on the papery operation gown, via miserable attempts at jokes about the cut-out paper dolls we made when we were young. Her phone rings. Her father. She mutes

169

it and gives it to me. The phone vibrates as we silently wait for the doctor. The damn thing won't stop. 'Life won't get out of my hair, will it?' she murmurs, and grabs the phone. 'Yes, Dad? Is it urgent? I have … a meeting …' Her eyes bulge, like sped-up footage of a carnation blooming. She hangs up and screams, 'Nuuurse!' Two nurses appear at the door. With one hand on her hip, the other slapping at the air, the classic pose of a Turkish woman going ballistic, she shouts, 'Who called my father? Who told my father about the fucking pregnancy? Answer me now!' The older nurse, apparently the more reasonable of the two, murmurs, 'Shit! They did it again.'

Three of us are by the bed now, the nurse holding one of her hands, me the other. Now the footage is of a dying carnation in slow motion. The nurse explains, with the appropriate curses interjected, 'As soon as you test positive at the laboratory they record it. They call you first. If they can't reach you, they call your husband and tell him about the pregnancy, and if you're single they call your father, regardless of your age. It's called "pregnancy health monitoring". But you see, they use it to prevent an abortion, in case you were planning to decide on such a thing, I mean, God forbid, on your own! It's been like that for a while now. And private clinics also have to report every abortion to the state. If you were married, you would have needed your husband's written approval as well. Otherwise there's a big fine for the clinic. The bastards do everything they can to keep their hands between our legs!'

We walk to the operation room door together in solidarity. I hand her over to the female doctor, and my friend cries openly now. The doctor hugs her.

Two hours later, in the hospital ward, we silently eat cake together. She constantly readjusts her papery outfit. It is 2014, and we look like the last scene from a very long documentary entitled *Termination: How to Create the Ideal Female Citizen for Your Dictatorship*.

Throughout history every societal, religious or political project has treated women like cut-out paper dolls, to be dressed in or stripped of the ruling power's chosen ideological outfit. From the Nazi Party's ideal woman's trinity '*Kinder, Küche, Kirche*', or Stalin's working-class hero 'New Soviet Woman', to today's career-driven-happily-married-with-children-flat-belly warrior woman, the drive to create paper dolls hasn't ceased. A woman's image, and sometimes her soul, is moulded and unmoulded, shaped according to the regime's taste and used as a store mannequin to promote the prevailing political power's concept of the ideal female citizen. Every regime, without exception, starts building its ideal citizen by tampering with its women. It takes a whole generation to create a new man, but redesigning women, so they believe, is an overnight job. And it is unfortunate that every one of these projects, despite their obvious hostility towards

171

women, is always able to find female supporters whose substance is as pliable as Play-Doh. It is no coincidence, therefore, that in every country currently experiencing a rise in right-wing populism, women are the first and most vocal people to react. They are the first to feel the poke of misogyny, which is the wingman to right-wing populism. Even those who choose to wait and see eventually realise that, when the authoritarian leader begins his march to power, sooner or later the question for all women becomes whether to accept becoming Play-Doh and sacrificing their dignity to gain the approval of the leader/*father*, or whether to enter into a bloody struggle that begins with them saying, 'Thanks, but no thanks.'

'Please think about it. We want to collaborate with women like you.'
It is 2009, and Erdoğan's regime is reluctantly trying to win the consent of seculars in Turkey for what will prove to be the last time, before it decides henceforth to design its own citizens, befitting of the new Turkey, and tell everyone else they're 'welcome to leave'. Obsessive repetition of the word 'empathy' has stripped it of meaning, and due to increased polarisation even the most minimal consensus is lacking from daily life. It's a time when 'only for seculars' or 'only for the religious' residential projects are advertised on billboards, the former out of fear, the latter with enthusiasm. The common social codes are gradually disappearing. Every

time a woman is harassed because she is wearing shorts, or a man is beaten because he is not fasting during the holy month of Ramadan, supporters of the government grin and say it's *an isolated incident* and shouldn't be exaggerated. It's not the perpetrators, but those who draw attention to the incident, who are blamed for polarising society, and for being disconnected from the values of real people. And whenever this kind of attack causes too much of a reaction, Erdoğan compassion-ately chastises his supporters, saying, 'This is wrong. We respect women.' Since he is above the law, nobody is entitled to ask him about his own contribution to increased polarisation and hostility towards secular women. Furthermore, his politicising of the legal system renders it irrelevant, leaving the country at his mercy and with a limited understanding of justice. It's a time when the regime slaps unsupportive women with one hand while repeatedly offering them an olive branch with the other; a dizzying time.

After receiving a number of insistent invitations, I finally attend an AKP women's branch board meet-ing. At the lavish party headquarters, a big, vibrantly coloured picture of Erdoğan, the great leader, domi-nates the room. The regional executives of the women's branch, some with and some without headscarves, are performing the 'having a regular meeting' act for me. The room feels like a girls' school classroom where all the students are conscientious, well-mannered and unnaturally content. It seems the only person from local politics is the head of the branch, a petite, anxious woman. The others look too serene to have had to struggle in a man's world. When the eerily peaceful meeting, with its curious air of perfect consensus, comes to an end, the head of the women's branch takes me into her room. All of a sudden the mood becomes a heart-to-heart. She says, 'We want to collaborate with women like you.' *Women like me* means women they cannot, and in fact should not, collaborate with: single, openly critical, leftist, independent, and all the other things deemed unfitting to a pious community. She tells me how every week they host a woman from *the other side*. Her trustworthy attitude makes it easy to imagine how many women might be convinced by this tempting offer of an olive branch in a climate where polarisation is destroying any sense of solidarity among women. The call for empathy feels like a truce after an exhausting struggle. However, it is far from clear whether I'm being invited to enter into a peace deal on equal terms, or being asked to surrender. So I say, 'Thanks, but no thanks.'

A few years later, Erdoğan appoints yet another woman as minister for women and family who believes that child marriages are 'actually innocent at heart'. By 2014, Erdoğan is confident enough that he won't be challenged at a pro-government women's rights groups summit to say, 'Our religion [Islam] has defined a position for women: motherhood. You cannot explain this to feminists because they don't accept the concept of motherhood.' The same year he lashes out against the contraceptive pill for being *treason against the country*. He dismisses abortion and caesarean-section deliveries as *homicide*. Nobody really understands why caesareans are wrong all of a sudden, but his words are enough to make hospitals apply *de facto* limitations on performing them. Murders of women have skyrocketed, and child marriages are being legitimised as 'our traditional values' promoted by Erdoğan and his party.

By 2017, every other day social media is shaken by a new video or photo of primary school girls dressed as mini ideal women, wearing headscarves and washing their male friends' feet at end of year ceremonies, or five-year-olds praying in their *chadors* around a pretend Mecca. And women like me find themselves forced to play the badass whenever our daily lives and our intimate parts are poked by the regime. We can hardly trust the state institutions to protect us against any kind of violation, unless we are among the few women or men who still manage to occupy state positions and risk their job by respecting its requirements rather than Erdoğan's words.

In 2016, mass production of the new female citizen – either by the transformation of existing ones or by bringing up a new generation through conservative education – is in full force, with the new specimens ready to be presented to the market: pious, obedient, docile, silent and largely confined to the home. The tolerance/empathy/dialogue phase is over, and now it's time to replace the old model with the new version. The good girls of the party have been waiting for a long time to take over every social position occupied by a secular woman – with the consent of their male guardians, of course. But hang on. If they want women to be good girls, all proper and conservative, what are a transgender woman and a sexy singer doing in President Erdoğan's palace, sitting at his table, breaking fast with him at Ramadan?

The photo was distributed to the national and international press. Bülent Ersoy, known as 'Diva', had a sex-change operation in 1981, and became the most well-known transgender person in Turkey. She is also an iconic figure in Turkish classical music, and the queen of flamboyant theatrical glamour. Together with Sibel Can, a former belly dancer and the most popular singer in Turkey, Diva chats away happily with Erdoğan and the first lady. The two women, seemingly from *the other side*, are smiling their proper girl smiles and gazing at Erdoğan as if in desperate need of his approval. It's the perfect photo for the new female citizen of Turkey: 'We don't necessarily ask you to change yourself, to wear a headscarf and that sort of thing. All we ask is for your full obedience and submission.' Or else …

This dinner takes place the day after the police use rubber bullets and tear gas to stop a gay pride parade in central Istanbul, at which the government's tolerance for hate killings was being protested against. Today, the TV channels are, naturally, showing Diva, with her never-ending obsequious praise for Erdoğan's manliness, rather than the undesirable version of transgender citizens. The only cast member missing from the regime's line-up at this point is an international presence. Somebody like, let's say, Lindsay Lohan.

'In Turkey you have free will as a woman. It's amazing here, you can do what you want and it's accepted,' says American movie star Lohan in October 2016. She is wearing a headscarf during her visit to Turkey as part of an arrangement clumsily designed to use her as publicity material for the Turkish government. As a matter of fact, she is right: so long as you praise Erdoğan ('He has a big heart,' she says), Turkey is a wonderful place to be a woman. It doesn't really matter if there are nude pictures of you circulating on social media. A headscarf can always be used to reset the past, and you can still be the poster girl for a pious authoritarian leader, used to promote *the cause. Stanno tutti bene!*

Meanwhile, in social and political circles, teachers, academics, MPs, state officials and civil servants are being replaced by party members, or the wives or daughters of party members, and mostly those in head-scarves. The groundwork for introducing the party's new ideal female citizen is laid in every sphere of life via new regulations. As Erdoğan and his cronies make life easy for *their kinda girl*, it gets harder and harder for all the other kinds to survive. Daily life becomes increasingly intimidating, and at times downright dangerous, for women who don't dress 'properly'. At one point, women collectively take to wearing shorts, out of solidarity with girls who've been beaten for wearing them. The nature of these attacks is so primitive that it leads to seemingly ridiculous acts of defiance, which are rarely discussed in the media, as attacks against the undesired version of the female citizen escalate so fast. However, the attacks do not only come from men encouraged by misogynistic regulations or statements made by the government. It is the new generation of female citizens, fired up with wrath thanks to the party's narrative, who actually perform the job best. Here is a story for those who cannot picture how merciless these 'proper daughters' with their new-found sense of entitlement can be when they are let off the leash by their leader/father.

'Well, since she committed suicide she must have been an atheist, so she goes to hell. One less social democrat vote anyway :)'

An AKP Youth Branch board member, a woman in her late twenties, wrote this on Twitter in April 2018.

(The smiley is her sense of humour, not my typo.) She was responding to the suicide of a female teacher who, like forty-three others among 439,000 jobless young teachers, killed herself out of despair. The AKP tweeter, the classic militant *party girl*, was around the same age as the teacher. Both grew up with the AKP in power; one turned out to be the regime's ideal girl, and the dead one didn't.

The AKP woman's attitude is not especially uncommon among party members and supporters. In fact, some TV anchormen only ever mention the killing of secular, disobedient people in passing. The female AKP member was wearing a headscarf, yes, but that was not the most significant or important part of her 'ideal' profile. Many women who wear headscarves protested against her evil post, while many female AKP supporters who do not wear headscarves shared the joke, adding their own smileys. It is not a simple polarisation, as the Western media likes to paint it, between covered and uncovered women. The distinction between these two groups of women is not about what they have on their heads, but what is *in* their heads. A wave of anger surged through social media after the young woman expressed her warped sense of joy. Many found themselves asking, not for the first time in recent years, 'When did you become so cruel?'

* * *

'*When did you become so cruel? A man died, a retired teacher, because of the excessive use of tear gas. And yet you sarcastically smile and say, "May he rest in peace! He shouldn't have challenged Erdoğan." Exactly when did you become such a person? You say, "He is our prime minister, he has charisma; he can do whatever he wants." When did you start to believe that? Listen up, and answer me. I'm asking you to name the exact year when you became such a person. I'm asking you to state when exactly you turned into … this!*'

This is me being *the brave writer coming down hard on the Erdoğan supporter* on the most well-known TV political debate show in Turkey, after the man had defended the unrestrained police violence meted out against opposition voices on 10 June 2011. From that day on, the question 'When did you become so cruel?' became something of a motto taken up by many others, and was repeated so many times that even several years later, if you typed the words in Turkish into Google, my face, twisted with anger, was the first thing to appear. The question probably sounded rhetorical to many people, themselves struggling with a similar sense of bewilderment before the rabid polarisation that had been manufactured between the ideal citizens of the regime and everyone else. But I really was asking him to specify the exact moment of his transformation, the moment when his basic human values became totally disfigured. The question was actually about when, or in what circumstances, human beings lose their basic sense of empathy towards other human beings, and instead become politically charged with antipathy.

Torturers, I learned early in my career as a journalist, thanks to Turkey's recent political history, are normal human beings. Sociopaths suffering from extreme antipathy are rare exceptions, and are not considered ideal candidates for the job. Although practising evil traumatises perpetrators as well as victims in the end, torturers live most of their lives as ordinary family men, with kids whom they hug after a long day at work. And every so often, when one of them confesses to his crimes, he mostly gives two reasons for the evil he committed. First, 'We had no choice, it was our job'; and then, if you dig a little deeper, the second reason comes to the surface: 'They were evil, and we wanted to eradicate evil from the country. We had a cause.'

Sooner or later, when their cause becomes outdated due to changes in the political landscape, they are left alone with the fact that it is *they* who are the embodiment of evil, and are obliged to live the rest of their lives with the knowledge that they lost a large part of their humanity for a cause that now seems nonsensical; *an art* not *easy to master*. That is when and why they start going around the media like miserable little beggars, desperate to confess, to be forgiven. They almost always speak in a low voice, for they know victims always recognise their torturers through their voice. They whisper when asking to be forgiven for their extreme antipathy.

Fascism, reads Madeleine Albright's book title, in big red letters, and the subtitle, *A Warning*. The former American secretary of state says she felt compelled to write the book not only because of the election of Donald Trump, but because she has observed a far bigger danger in terms of the current political and social *zeitgeist*, and she does not hesitate to call it fascism. With her students at Princeton University, she explores the symptoms of the current political and social malaise in the US, and tries to conceptualise them. One of the three main ways fascism takes hold, she says, is by 'pushing away the empathy'. One wonders how much empathy might have been required in the world where Albright was one of the main political figures, in what she apparently considers to have been better times. Or to put it another way, how much antipathy is normal and legitimate in a neo-liberal system where the winner takes all and, as we saw in the post-truth chapter, appears to feel no shame for the unjust distribution of – well, pretty much everything, justice included? Who is it that can draw the red line between the normal antipathy that's required to get by in these times and the excessive antipathy that turns a human into a fascist, an *antipathy militia*?

*   *   *

'He's dying anyway.'

In the first week of May 2018, mainstream American media experienced a sort of empathy frenzy. All news outlets were deeply concerned about a leak from a White House staff meeting. Republican Senator John McCain, a strong critic of Trump and a war hero to many Americans, a political figure considered untouchable, had brain cancer, and somebody from the Trump administration, while trashing McCain's criticism, had apparently said, 'He's dying anyway.' For almost a week, TV channels and newspapers anxiously waited for an apology from the White House. Several times one version or another of my question was asked in TV debates: 'When did you become so cruel?' Discussions centred around concern about what kind of people Trump supporters were. There was a growing concern that the values being promoted by the White House would spread through the entire country, and create a new type of citizen: a bully seething with antipathy. Despite desperate calls for an apology, the response from the White House remained stone cold: 'We prefer not to discuss a leak from a staff meeting.' At the time, I, and doubtless many others like me, thought, so what if they apologise? Would that automatically make the members of Trump's White House good people? Would an apology suffice to turn things around?

*　*　*

The difficulty for those fighting for democracy, who don't have a problem with neoliberal values *per se*, is that they don't have a good story to tell about their ideals for human beings. Because in order to promote a political goal you need an intact narrative with a good character, an ideal citizen to put forward as the mannequin of your system's ethical stance. That's why, when they are asked the crucial questions, they either go mute or talk too much to conceal the fact that they are not saying anything. Because the crucial questions are: 'Who is the good human being in *your* story?' 'Who is *your* ideal heroic citizen?' 'What are *your* guy's or woman's wonderful values?'

Humans are incapable of functioning and living together without a good story to bind them and keep a certain set of values intact. That's why the lack of a story in neoliberalism, the lack of *meaning and cause*, can be unbearable for the human mind. Since humans are forced to live in a state of mild antipathy – an acceptable amount of antipathy that is crucial to the neoliberal system – they are forever in dire need of a cause, a central triangulation point that they can use to orientate themselves in relation to what's good and what's bad. The ethical vacuum of neoliberalism, its dismissal of the fact that human nature needs meaning and desperately seeks reasons to live, creates fertile ground for the invention of *causes*, and sometimes the most groundless or shallowest ones. Contrary to what those who defend the system believe, the desire to have more, or the fear of having less, can never fill the void in a human mind. And it has always been the easy way out to call North Koreans, Al Qaeda or ISIS 'crazy people', but this is a failure to recognise that a cause and its ability to provide meaning can be more powerful than any war machine man has ever made. It is therefore possible to see right-wing populism as providing neoliberalism with its cause. The masses' desperate craving is met with a simple story in which the villain is obvious: the elite, the witch women, the foreigners, the traitors, or whoever. That is why, although established politicians complain about right-wing populism, in fact the movement is like a prosthesis for neoliberalism's missing story, with its wonderfully intact *cause/meaning*. People's desire for a cause is satisfied by the authoritarian leader's confidently told story. However, the villain of this story is not necessarily only found among the ranks of the authoritarian leaders.

'When I see Mark Zuckerberg with his T-shirts and jeans and trainers, I always think of Umberto Eco saying fascism doesn't always show up in uniform. Now we know it can also appear in casual wear.'

In April 2018 I was in Berlin giving one of the keynote speeches at Re:publica, Europe's largest festival focused on digital life and politics. I was talking about the ideal citizen according to a neoliberal set of values.

For a very long time, the cut-out paper dolls of the neo-liberal system, the ideal citizens and therefore humanity's pioneers, were T-shirt- and hoodie-wearing high-tech personalities. Ever since Steve Jobs, they'd become the highly admired prophets of the new world, and their revelations were eagerly awaited in order to quench the desperate thirst for knowledge and advancement. Whenever they were ready to reveal their wisdom, in other words their latest new gadgets, their appearances would be celebrated with spectacular shows broadcast worldwide, as if a message from on high was being transmitted through them to us mere mortals. At first it was all good and it all seemed clean, white-iPod clean. But then Mark Zuckerberg happened.

In the beginning, Facebook was heralded as an important bond that would bring humanity together, and we would await Mr Zuckerberg's latest revelation as if the head of the UN were about to make a statement that would change the future of the planet. However, during the American Senate hearing on unauthorised data selling in April 2018, the ideal citizen of our times turned out to be – surprise, surprise – a young man seeking profit who didn't really care much about truth, politics or the good of humanity.

So perhaps it is no surprise that over the last decade or so, the new generation of internet pioneers, together with campaigners for good causes in need of promotion, have come up with carefully-designed, apolitical, 'socially responsible' campaigns aimed at providing a 'cause' to fill the big emptiness, the moral void at the heart of the global communication network. Perhaps the most famous of these was the 'Ice Bucket Challenge' for motor neurone disease, which was taken up by many around the world, from sports stars to politicians. The prophets offered fun games to humanity, which, despite their proliferation across the web, were pitifully insubstantial in terms of effecting any real change. They were a form of global communication in which very little was actually being communicated, and were desperately inadequate in terms of providing people with a lasting cause. And so we witnessed once again the dictum that holds true for both nature and politics: *Horror vacui* – the abhorrence of a vacuum. The vacuum inside the global network was successfully filled by serious-sounding great 'causes', as defined by right-wing leaders.

The numerous new gadgets and communication platforms did not necessarily promote right-wing populism, but, like a fallow field, the human mind had been left uncultivated through decades of depoliticisation, and this in turn provided fertile ground for those who claimed to have a cause to propagate. It turned out that it is not enough just to connect people in order to try to create empathy. The ones who had a 'real' cause – whether it was Trump, Putin or Erdoğan – took the void at the heart of the world wide web and gleefully filled it, turning people into militants of antipathy. They said to their followers: 'Nobody cares about you, so you don't have to care about anybody. *They're dying anyway.*' They systematically manipulated the grudges and the anger of the neglected masses, turning them into a xenophobic and hostile political narrative. These militants became the ideal citizens of right-wing populism, people who could say, 'He's dying anyway,' or 'He deserves to die if he's standing in the way of the cause.' And the only antidote offered against this powerful political and ethical poison was Google's nice, sweet motto: 'Don't be evil.'

But how should we be, then? Which direction is evil coming from? What *is* the cause that will connect people to keep them morally intact? Where are we all supposed to be heading? You don't know? Well, they do. Or they think they do, which is more than enough.

'There is our cause,' Erdoğan has said, again and again, over the years, 'and there are those who stand in the way …' The content of the cause that he brought to Turkish politics has never been made clear. During his sixteen years in power, Erdoğan has never actually defined or explained what this cause is, although it became clear over time that he wants not only an Islamic and ultra-conservative Turkey, but also an authoritarian regime in which even children are subjected to severe politicisation, obliged to show total obedience to the ruler, and thus become his ideal citizens.

* * *

'*The necessary arrangements have been made and kindly submitted for your consideration, sir.*'

23 April is 'National Sovereignty and Children's Day' in Turkey, marking the anniversary of the founding of Parliament in 1920. There is a tradition that all high-level state offices are handed over to children for the day, and the officials pretend to be their deputies. The symbolism is that the children get to run the country temporarily because they represent the future. In 2010, this delightful custom became an embarrassing experience for the then prime minister Erdoğan. The badass little girl who was made PM for the day gave a statement to the press about democracy, and then took questions from journalists. When she was asked about the presidential system that Erdoğan had started pushing for at the time, she said, 'I am sorry to say I don't agree with the prime minister. Turkey is a democracy and it should continue being one.' Erdoğan giggled nervously, and there was a cold stillness in the room.

Eight years later, on 23 April 2018, a little boy was sitting in the presidential chair and the press questions were about to start. Before any were asked, Erdoğan looked towards the education minister and asked with his eyes whether everything was under control. The minister said, 'The necessary arrangements have been ...' The kid had been vetted and instructed by his elders, and he answered the questions just as he'd been told to, with memorised lines and a text previously cleared by the party. But the most striking image of the day was the nine-year-old girl who took over the seat of the head of Parliament – she was wearing a headscarf. The photo that was distributed to the press was a perfect depiction of proud fathers whose daughters were entirely products of their own creation: the girl in the middle, on either side of her the real head of Parliament and prime minister, and behind her Erdoğan with both hands resting on her shoulders, as if to exhibit the child as his bounty in a political war called *the cause*. Older versions of her were already cruel enough to mock, in the name of the cause, the suicide of a desperate woman, and now her time had come. She would be raised to acquire the antipathy towards her fellow citizens that the party required of her.

When I looked at that photo I wondered whether the cause would still be there when she grew up, or whether she'd be embarrassed by the photo, like anyone whose cause becomes outdated as a result of changes to the political landscape. In any case, the political symbolism of the photo was too heavy a burden for the shoulders of a little girl. She wasn't a pro like Lindsay Lohan, and she wasn't grown-up enough to know that her headscarf was actually part of a giant flag. For Erdoğan and his supporters, every headscarf in Turkey is woven into a bigger, magical flag, a flag that they use to manufacture crude tension between the model female citizen and all other women.

It is used to obscure the class differences between party supporters, and to hide the fact that the party's very own bourgeoisie is filthy rich. It is a flag that they wave before each election to extract political capital from female supporters, stirring sentiment by saying, 'Our sisters with headscarves have been humiliated.' It is a flag under which all the ideal women of the regime can be brought together, leaving the less than ideal ones in the corner of the unwanted.

'You'd better sit over on the other side, Ms Temelkuran.'
I believe in monkish toil when it comes to writing. After sitting at the same desk, staring at the same wall, listening to the same music on repeat and wearing the same lousy cardigan for months, you finally bore yourself into finishing off what you're working on. But there are times when the body rebels and screams, 'Sorry luv, get me out of here!' – and so I go outside to work.

Emirgan Park is one of the most beautiful places on the Bosporus, with its big chalet dating back to the Ottoman era. However, on that particular day in the spring of 2014, when I entered the park with my laptop, I noticed it was full of high-end cars: Porsches, Ferraris, Bentleys, Hummers, nothing below a Mercedes S Class. As I stood in the chalet's crowded garden I saw a 'headscarves-only convention' of some sort. The women were all dripping from head to toe with luxury brands. Either because of my shabby appearance or the fact that I was not one of them, I felt a sense of mild intimidation. I was the intruder, it seemed, a trespasser, a woman from the other side. The waiter, who apparently not only recognised my face but knew my political stance, and so realised the awkwardness of the situation, walked over to me, trying to hide a smile. My raised eyebrows were enough for him to offer me the full political context: 'It's been like this for a while. It's *their* place now. Only the rich ones, of course.' He told me that several chalets on both sides of the Bosporus had become meeting points for *party girls*, the female *nouveau riche*, where they enjoyed the delights of the New Ottomanism that had been one of the components of Erdoğan's *cause*. The waiter gently ushered me away to an isolated corner, saying, 'You'd better sit over on the other side, Ms Temelkuran.'

The false dichotomy of the clash between the ideal woman and the unideal one has been manufactured according to party tastes: 'the mean girl' (secular, disobedient) and 'the bullied girl' (loyal to the party). However, this engineered catfight does not necessarily require an outfit; most of the time a few willing and unwilling cats will suffice.

'We're not standing in the shadows any more! We won't be pushed around by bullies telling us who we're "supposed" to …'

Although it sounds like the beginning of a statement from the #MeToo movement, or a declaration of intent from an oppressed minority, this battle cry was actually the intro to the womenvotetrump.com manifesto in 2018. The website was announcing – after years of unbearable suppression that nobody, including the movement's members, was aware of until 2017 – that they would not be silent any more. They were particularly enraged after comedian Michelle Wolf roasted White House press secretary Sarah Huckabee Sanders during the White House Correspondents' Dinner, an annual event at which the political journalists of DC mock the president and the White House staff, and vice versa, through humorous stage speeches. Throughout her speech, Wolf, in this case representing the capital's political elite, came down hard on the White House's spokesperson; Sanders had to sit there and take it as all the accumulated anger her role as Trump's mouthpiece had generated was poured out on her.

The next morning, a particularly American kind of catfight between ideal female citizens and all other women was simmering and ready to be served. The flag for this controversy was not the headscarf but banners declaring 'humility against meanness' waved by female Trump supporters. On Fox TV and other supportive media, the bullied Trump women heralded a new dawn of resistance. Using the language of high school to stoke the controversy, Trump-supporting women branded

Wolf as 'the mean girl', while Sanders' cool attitude on the night was praised as 'the class act'. It was another nice polarisation that created a cause, or the illusion of a cause, and which, inevitably, spawned its own female role models.

'Who wouldn't want their daughter to be like Ivanka Trump?'

This is another quote from the Trump-supporting women's website. For the production line of female role models to get into full swing, the leader needs to offer a blueprint for the ideal female citizen. Just as Ivanka Trump (in her father's words 'a woman with a perfect body') was promoted as the ideal woman in the early days of the Trump administration, so Erdoğan's daughter Sümeyye was championed in the first years of her father's rule. Who wouldn't want their daughter to be like Sümeyye Erdoğan in the new Turkey? A pious, well-educated but obedient young woman who would do anything for her father, for the leader, for the cause – or whatever her father says the cause is.

And if you say how ridiculous this all is, especially knowing that these party girls sit on millions of dollars because of nepotism, you might, God forbid, offend these women and become 'the mean girl'. Once the moral high ground has been seized, it's not easy to get it back, even if you are very, very politically correct.

* * *

'So you see no problem, politically ... or ethically?'

The news about Trump's alleged payment of hush money to one or several porn stars accompanies his cancellation of the Iran nuclear deal live across the TV networks on 7 May 2018. The screens are a mass of mumbo-jumbo. On CNN International, a woman from *the other side* is paired in a live discussion with a female Trump supporter. The decorum hardly holds as the Trumpette repeatedly says, 'Well, we didn't vote for him for his personal life.'

The woman on the other side keeps to rhetorical questions so as not to overstep the line into 'causing offence' – quite a severe limitation in American social and political life. As she continues to ask about 'funnelling' the hush money – this being a repeated act in Trump's case – and whether silencing women with money is ethical or not, the Trumpette keeps saying the same thing: 'We believe he's doing a good job for us, and that's what matters.' So the one-sided debate leads down a cul de sac where there is no argument other than 'He's our guy, and you can't understand that because you won't share our cause' versus 'We cannot understand how you are not embarrassed.' The woman from *the other side* eventually stops asking questions, so as not to be 'the mean girl'. The anchorwoman smiles helplessly. The understated call for the Trumpette to feel embarrassed falls on deaf ears, and 'the class act' once again sticks to her unknown cause.

That same day I have a book event in Portland, Oregon. I talk about how a collapse of global morals is visible in political terms, and how we can survive it by appreciating the history of the problem. As always, a number of questions from the audience centre around my personal situation: my living in Zagreb, being 'self-exiled', etc. A woman finally asks the classic question, 'Do you feel in danger?' I smile and reply, 'No offence, but' – when in Rome! – 'do *you* feel in danger? You have a president who grabs women, after all.' The global attack on women, and the connected attempt by right-wing populism to reshape them into characters from *The Handmaid's Tale*, excludes no nationality, no social class, no religion and no privilege. She nods with concern. 'They start with women, with the "weak", you know,' I continue. 'And then they carry on with the others.' She comes up to me during the book signing afterwards, and talks about the polarisation among American women, and how appalling it is. 'I don't understand the reason, I mean, what the main cause is,' she says. And I simply respond, 'Maybe we don't have to understand the reason, or the cause for that matter. Maybe there's nothing to understand there.'

Because the answer to the question 'When did you become so cruel?', whether it's being asked by Americans, Germans or any other country's citizens, is that these people changed the day their leader mentioned or insinuated a *cause*. As long as there is a cause, and the leader is then able to draw a line between those who are for and those who are against it, there is no ethical crime humans won't resort to. This is something we can see just by looking at history. The current twist to the experience is that with new right-wing populist movements there actually is no solid, noble, so-called cause, no written manifesto they feel tied to, or ideological narrative they use as a cover-up – nothing other than the lust for power.

Robert O. Paxton, in his 2005 book *The Anatomy of Fascism*, says that neither Hitler nor Mussolini had clear and definite party programmes, and so they could reshape their formless political movements whenever necessary. However, at least the authoritarian leaders of the twentieth century had an ideological starting point, some sort of 'ism' that they operated under, as opposed to today's autocrats, who mention no ideology by name. What they have are their personal promises and their ever-changing goals. Therefore, their supporters must be shown what to do, how they are supposed to transform themselves to fit the leader's requirements. With each redirection of policy they have to work out how to behave so as not to end up in the wrong category of citizen. Their only North Star, the only guide they have to follow in this ever-changing political environment, is the unquestioned leader. Information concerning swift changes en route to the so-called cause is transmitted using the dog whistle that connects the leader to his supporters. In this new environment, political inconsistency or lack of integrity not only become insignificant, but also, through quick changes in discourse, allow the ruler to make his critics dizzy, and hesitant even to name this new phenomenon. This, of course, leaves those people on *the other side*, the undesirable citizens, wavering.

'But aren't we supposed to understand *why*? Aren't we supposed to get into a dialogue with these people and try to understand their cause?' asks a female American student after another one of my university talks in May 2018. I find myself saying no, a clear and definite no, and I ask back, 'Do you, or do we, really make the same effort to understand or to talk to "our own kind", so to speak? When was the last time you spoke to progressives to try to understand *their* cause?' She falls silent. I try to elaborate: had all the effort wasted on trying to understand populist leaders' supporters been put to use in speaking to *the other side*, that's to say your own side, maybe things would have turned out differently. Over the course of the discussion it had become clear that members of the audience had not read half as many news stories about Bernie Sanders as about Donald Trump. And eventually we agree that there is not as much news about what Sanders voters feel or think as there is about Trumpeters. To keep on staring at the words and acts of the ruler/perpetrator is to be a rabbit stuck in the headlights, to forget that you can actually take steps to avoid what's hurtling towards you. And I say to the students, 'Rabbits don't think. A rabbit either takes that first step and runs to protect itself … or it doesn't.'

'Do you remember what that "famous" troll said in his TV interview? You've forgotten, of course. So many things have happened in recent years. He said, "We wanted to start with making women less strong, and see what happened. It was only an experiment." Don't you remember?'

This is Aylin Aslım speaking, a songwriter, an amazingly beautiful woman and a political one. And yeah, she's also a rock star. We are in northern Spain with friends. After things got messy in Turkey, some of us started living abroad temporarily, while others, like Aylin, moved to secluded coastal towns in Turkey. We avoid talking about our defeat and retreat in order not to spoil the short vacation and the limited time we get to spend together, away from the depressing muddle of Turkish politics. She was the first of us to be attacked by government supporters, and at one point social media was filled with threats that they would turn up at her concerts with machetes, or publicly advertise her phone number and home address in case anyone wanted to attack her in person, while at the same time her name trended with an assortment of lies that turned her into the mother of all evils.

We rarely talk about what has really happened to us in the last few years, how our lives have been damaged, because badass women don't do that – we survive. But now, in another country and several years later, she tells me her heart was broken. Not by the attacks themselves, but by her friends' silence, and by the general meaninglessness of the cruel acts committed against her. 'When a woman is attacked and is not the sister or wife of someone powerful, there is this strange silence. Nobody wants to get his or her hands dirty. They expect you to get out of the swamp on your own, and it's impossible. The most horrible thing is there's no reason for it, you know? They ruined my life just as an experiment, just as practice, before they did the same thing to more established women.'

They don't make political heroes out of women, apart of course from dead ones. Women are hardly ever chosen to be the symbols of resistance, to mobilise the opposition. And that's exactly why the authoritarian regimes start with women. Character assassinations, or any other kind of violation committed against female opposition figures or women deemed undesirable citizens by the regime, rarely trigger a united reaction among dissidents, and the regime knows this. That is why many do not know the name of Claudette Colvin, who refused to sit at the back of a segregated bus nine months prior to Rosa Parks. As an unwed, pregnant teenager, she would have been deemed easy fodder for segregationists, and she wasn't considered respectable enough to be a figurehead for the civil rights movement.

So maybe it's more important to urgently build bonds of solidarity, without scrutinising how respectable the victim is, than it is to try to understand the reason for the attacks on her. These are attacks, after all, that turn us into the regime's paper dolls, or the first experiments towards them. The victim is not only a victim because she is attacked, but also because she carries the burden of failing to understand the perpetrator. Not because of any desperate need for empathy, but because she needs to give meaning to what has happened to her. But radical evil, inasmuch as we've failed as human beings to understand it so far, does not require a particular reason. Even if it did, trying to understand it should be the perpetrator's burden. After thousands of hearts and lives were broken in Turkey, we, as women, understood this: they want us to be just like them, end of story. And the only meaningful defence by which we can protect ourselves and each other is by building bonds of solidarity in order to change the political atmosphere and render it outdated, an evil cause that was no more than a passing trend.

'A society that is run for profit is destined to fail.'

Two days after my event in Oregon, on 9 May 2018, I see a local newspaper, the *Willamette Week*, in my hotel lobby. On its front page a young woman is shouting through a megaphone. The headline reads:

'The Socialist Network'. According to the long article about Olivia Katbi Smith, aged twenty-six, who managed to rally fast-food workers to unionise, the first fast-food-restaurant unionisation in the country, there is a strange new political wave in the city.

> Between January 2016 and today, the number of Oregonians who tick the 'not a member of any party' box when registering to vote increased by 58 per cent, while the number of Democrats increased by just 15 per cent. That is a telling indication of how young voters view politics. They are looking for something new. Something like the Democratic Socialists of America (DSA). The DSA is not a recognised political party, yet its meetings regularly attract as many as two hundred people. Democratic Party meetings in Portland, by comparison, draw a hundred people, usually retirees. The Republican Party of Portland pulls in around fifteen.

In the newspaper piece, Olivia tells the story of her transformation: how Obama bailed out the banks after 2008, how she realised that the Democrats of the establishment 'only throw bones to the poor', and how the party is really no different from the Republicans. She is one of the young women who made 'socialism' the most looked-up term on Wikipedia in the USA in 2016.

She is the new-generation left. As I look at her picture, I see the face of a young woman remembering something she can't even remember forgetting: that she is a capable political subject, and that politics actually runs on bread and butter – a crucial piece of memory that got erased in the 1980s. She is remembering what her mother, like the secular aunties in Turkey, was forced to forget. She is one of the thousands of women around the world using the *zeitgeist* of girl power to politicise and organise people in order to demand social justice. They understand that the established political parties will be of no use in pushing the new agenda of the left. She is, in fact, there to remind everyone around her what the progressives in her country forgot during the 1980s: that there is an alternative. She is the new kind of woman who might actually challenge the cut-out dolls of the authoritarian regime, unlike conventional critics with their hesitant questions on Democrats-versus-Trumpettes TV debates. Because she has answers, she has a counter-cause to challenge right-wing populism's illusion of a cause. She is the rabbit taking that step.

'So you think there's hope?'
Every time I finish a talk about the state of the world, whether it's in Turkey or in other European or American cities, there's always a minute or two of awkward silence afterwards, accompanied by sighs of desperation that make me feel like the Cassandra of our

times. Then comes the first question, which is almost always: 'So, is there any hope?' I have memorised an answer whereby I say, 'Hope is a fragile word. I prefer to believe in determination, the determination to create beauty, political beauty.' Sometimes there happens to be a particularly determined person in the audience who asks, 'So where is the hope?' My answer is always the same: 'Follow the young women.'

At this time in human history we, as women, are empowered as never before. But more importantly, this is the first time in human history that women are learning not to be afraid or embarrassed about being more powerful than men. This new generation of women, women who grew up not with Cinderella stories but on *The Hunger Games* and *Mad Max 2*, are ready to break the truce that allowed men to dominate the political establishment. They have realised that it wasn't a peace accord signed on equal terms, but an undignified surrender. This is one of the reasons people in many places talk of a crisis of masculinity, and why, in the US, men of the alt-right talk about their 'right' to have sex with women. And it's also why misogyny is an integral part of rising right-wing populism all around the Western world. It's a growing tension that increasingly feels like a war that is brewing, a war that's beyond party politics and conventional political factions. A big war for tiny demands.

* * *

'Well, I fight because I want to go to work during the week and to tango on Saturdays.'

It is 2003. The economic crisis in Argentina is ruining lives, but also bringing about new forms of solidarity, forcing the middle and lower classes to bond and create the kind of carnivalesque political resistance that I will explore in the next chapter. People are inventing their own money, they are forming goods exchange markets, and the streets are filled with protesters. I am on a very-early-morning train that has no windows, lying on the bench with a packet of rice under my head. The rice is for one of the *piqueteros*, the barricaders. The protesters have been closing off the main arteries into Buenos Aires, building barricades to stop the city's life flow and wielding metal sticks with which they fight the police every day. I am going to meet one of the neighbourhood leaders, a petite twenty-four-year-old woman, a single mother with a one-year-old and a gentle soul who speaks in a low voice. She has a little hut with an earthen floor. She brings me *mate*, the only thing she has to offer a guest. We talk about the country, the excruciating life conditions endured by poor women, how she bundles up her baby while fighting the police. After an hour, I finally ask her why she does it, what she expects from the future. 'To go to work during the week and to tango …'

She does not expect to change the world, she does not speak about a global revolution, she just wants a decent life – and that is her *cause*. The demand seems tiny, but it leads her to physically fight the political powers and to risk her baby's life. Some call her a terrorist, and she is certainly not some people's idea of the desired female citizen. And although her demand sounds small, she is obliged to fight a big fight to get it.

I have often thought about that young Argentinian woman in recent years, because her face keeps reappearing before me, in different shapes and colours, wherever I go. A new kind of woman is emerging as a political reaction to both the right-wing movement's wingman misogyny and the hesitation of her sisters to engage with conventional politics. This new woman very rarely features in televised debates or appears in the mainstream media, but I keep running into her in every country I go to. She does not meander around the political discourse; she knows that you can only fight against a cause with another cause. She does not demand power, indeed she rejects it. She wants a decent life for everyone, and she knows that political polarisation and the hostile policies of the political powers cannot be dealt with using couples therapy techniques like empathy. Like the statue of the little girl outside the New York Stock Exchange, she is not afraid of the bulls or the bullies. And most importantly, she no longer believes in the current system of law, rather she believes in justice. She is no 'mine donkey' either.

* * *

'*You were the mine donkey*,' says a woman in a 'members only' club dining room in London in April 2018. Through an old friend, I've been invited to meet the new Turkish diaspora, all of them very rich women. They are around my age, extremely well educated, some are social democrats and some may be centre-right. It has been only a matter of weeks since they arrived in London, but they have all already bought houses in wealthy neighbourhoods. Their nannies and maids are hired through the informal 'relocation agencies' which have been turned into an emerging industry in several European cities by upper-class Turkish exiles since the military coup attempt of 2016 and the never-ending curfew that followed. Some of the diaspora have already re-established their businesses in London, while others are still researching their options.

I accepted the invitation because I thought it would be interesting to observe the world of these privileged immigrants; and it was. My gentle questions soon turn the chic dinner appointment into a group therapy session on the despairs of living abroad. One of them says, 'I love London, but I am nobody here, and I don't know this feeling. It is so new to me.' For years she was an executive in a multinational company in Turkey. Another talks about the hairdresser problem – not the fact that European cities lack good hairdressers, but her sense of not being treated like a princess the way we all were in Turkish salons. One of them reveals that she changed her name after she arrived in London: 'I never liked my name, so I thought, since this is a new life, now I can have a new name.' When their list of traumas moves on to the manicure issue – the Brits simply do not know how to manicure – my presence suddenly makes their problems feel embarrassingly insignificant. One of them says compassionately, 'Of course, compared to what you've been through ...' And then another adds, 'You were the mine donkey.' It's a Turkish expression, equivalent to 'canary in a coal mine', and a reference to the donkeys the military used to walk through minefields. Naturally, most of the donkeys ended up being blown up, much as these women thought I had.

So I steer the conversation back to the past, to the first years of Erdoğan and his new bourgeoisie. One by one they tell stories about how welcoming they, as the established, secular business class, had been to the new situation, and how they thought things would turn out differently. One of them, who is a leadership coach, says she even coached one AKP official to become a more effective leader, 'and he truly was a good person, I mean good at heart'. The confessions end with, 'We believed there would be dialogue. Of course we never thought it would come to this.'

'This' means a country where their daughters cannot go to a truly secular secondary school, where businesses are confiscated from one day to the next if someone accuses their owner of being a terrorist, where a woman can be attacked for what she wears on the street, a country where they cannot even write what they think on their Facebook pages for fear of imprisonment. 'Well, you know, it was the Kurdish women and the socialist women who were attacked first. It took a good many years before it came to *this*,' I say. And now *this* means them sitting in London talking about what happened, having said nothing until the oppression reached them, and then having the freedom to leave the country when it did. The dessert menu comes to their rescue. And all I can say is, 'Feeling like a nobody is good for the human soul. It's educational.' We exchange polite smiles and they start talking about their club memberships in London. It's a new phenomenon for them, but something they've already figured out they need in order to become somebodies in this country; their way of learning how it feels to be an oppressed member of a political minority.

'I ... have ... no place ... now ... to bury ... another ... child.'

The words barely come out of her; it's as if she's not speaking, but chewing on glass. We are in a secluded corner of UCLA in the summer of 2018. She is a Kurdish academic, an anthropologist, I am the book-touring Turkish writer, and we are clandestinely smoking on the smoke-free campus. I am constantly expecting some campus authority figure to spring out of nowhere and shout at us, but she couldn't care less. 'I am a Kurd,' she says, smiling, which in this context means, 'I don't give a damn after all I've been through.' After years of struggle, we are both now in a country where our stories are lost in translation. As a member of Kurdish intellectual circles, she was one of the first to suffer the oppression, and eventually had to leave the country. In 2016 there came a time when the government's anti-terror attacks in the south-eastern part of Turkey, a mostly Kurdish region, were so relentless that people couldn't go outside to bury the bodies of the dead. They had to live with them at home, putting dead babies in freezers. That's why we speak with tiny words, in half sentences. 'It is difficult to speak,' she says. 'It is difficult, yes,' I reply. So we smoke three cigarettes in a row, each of us looking in a different direction. Because that's what women do when they already know what it's like to be a nobody. You don't speak about it. And in the end you don't look like the characters in *The Handmaid's Tale*, but more like fading silhouettes that don't like to talk much. True pain doesn't have a pretty photo or a fancy TED story. True pain makes you truly want to become *a nobody* and stay away from the *admiring bog* that loves exiled-women stories; the bog Emily Dickinson once wrote about.

Only a few days after this conversation between two nobodies, Erdoğan said, 'Freedom, justice and democracy' when listing his election promises for 2018, after sixteen years in power. As soon as he made the statement his inner circle began to change its arrogant attitude. Clearly, even they were aware that the ideal citizen design programme was no longer working out for getting elected. One of the party's role models, a senior consultant to Erdoğan who kicked a mineworker after the Soma mine disaster of 2014 because the man had lost a relative and was asking for justice, suddenly made a public apology for his repulsive act. An apology much like the one the American people had waited in vain for the White House to issue regarding Senator John McCain.

Although the AKP's main figures had for years not hesitated to call upon their supporters to verbally and sometimes physically attack their critics, now they were putting on their election faces. Erdoğan, as always, placed himself above the law, and told everyone that he personally promised there would be more justice for those who didn't fit the party's idea of the ideal citizen. And in a matter of days the party's cruellest characters were reshaping themselves as easily as Play-Doh figures, becoming normal human beings apparently capable of empathy, as if such a thing were possible. For those who cannot picture the weirdness of this act, it's more or less like Trump, after years of praising white supremacists, suddenly holding up a Black Lives Matter placard in the run-up to an election. When there is a cause, and that cause is limited to a lust for power, content becomes so irrelevant that even the cruellest among us can pretend to be Santa Claus for a certain period of time, for the good of the cause. And those who not only reject the Christmas gifts but call the whole thing out as a crime against human dignity, and political power's latest attempt to remodel citizens according to the party's designs, become orphans of their own country.

In the summer of 2018, I covered some of the topics in this chapter in a speech to an audience of around 150 people at Stanford University. This included the routine about hope that I mentioned earlier, but still a young woman from the audience stood up, smiled and asked the question anyway: 'So let me ask you once again, is there hope?' I laughed, and answered, 'Let's say there is no hope. But there's still you and me, woman!' I guess that's enough, maybe more than enough. And sometimes it's all we have.

SIX

Let Them Laugh at the Horror

'The only difference between Guantánamo and last night was that the victims were praying the torture wouldn't stop.'

Around the brunch table my friends roll their eyes ostentatiously, but I couldn't care less. What's more delicious, I wonder: the walnut jam they've brought from Turkey, or my freshly-squeezed morning-after revenge? Last night they forced me out of my Zagreb bunker in order to quash my homesick blues by having 'fun'. Which is why I'm now unleashing my morning-person artillery. I expound upon the pacifying effects of electronic music and its heartbeat rhythm, ponder the neoliberal system's tendency to replace fun with joy, and, of course, lament the demise of dance music, the evolution that has led it to its current tragic state,

a halfway house between catatonia and drooping. I
embellish my description of the night as much as I can:
flashing lights designed to trigger mass epileptic fits, a
hammering noise that sounded like a tried-and-tested
method of sleep-deprivation torture, and an uncommu-
nicative crowd wobbling about in curious synchrony
like possessed members of some idiotic religious cult.
No real dancing, no laughter, no interaction between
people.

But my friends insist that I just don't get it. Two of
them, forty-something professional festival-goers with
Burning Man badges of honour to their name, keep
telling me that the best way to enjoy this carnivalesque
fun is by joining the *chemical brotherhood*, that those
blank eyes I saw were actually people high on MDMA
or ecstasy, and therefore filled with *joy*. 'My point
exactly,' I reply. 'All those people were mere atomised
units travelling in separately enhanced realities, each
one totally incapable of connecting with one another.
How convenient for today's world! And by the way,
pretending to have fun on such a massive scale is just
a manifestation of our lost capacity to experience joy.
And another thing …' The table finally attacks back
with their classic argument: 'You control freak, you're
afraid of letting go, of embracing the carnival spirit!'

I set my cutlery to one side. 'That, my friends, is
bullshit. I am the goddamn Cinderella of carnival, *real*
carnival, that is! As you know full well.'

And they do know. Because, since the summer of 2013, we have often found ourselves repeating the same thing: *We were all there, goddamn it!*

The hem of my long skirt is tucked into my belt, my shirt is wrapped around my face, and I'm running through the streets of Ankara wearing only one shoe. It's the night of 31 May 2013, only two days after mass protests broke out in Istanbul and inspired the entire country to join a carnivalesque resistance movement against a decade-old oppressive regime. In Ankara, clumsy, hastily-built barricades shut off all roads leading to Swan Park in the city centre. Young people who in the past have at most lit a few beach fires are now building bonfires to celebrate an uprising. The police have just sprayed tear gas, and I lost one of my ballet slippers as I ran away rubbing my eyes.

It's a funny fact about humanity: fear and pain, rather than courage and joy, are diminished when they are shared, and so I, like hundreds of people around me, am laughing as painful gas-tears run down my cheeks and as the tarmac hurts my bare foot. A man with a scarf wrapped around his face is yelling at me through the chaos of the fleeing crowd: 'Hey, you! I've got your shoe! Keep running!' Eventually we stop, and the guy uncovers his face. He turns out to be someone I knew several years ago. 'Here you go,' he says as he gives me my ballet slipper. 'Cinderella of the revolution!' Our faces are reconfigured, shaped by a previously unknown sort of laughter that rises from our innards and grips our features. We hug. I am not entirely sure we have hugged before. We swap speedy info about ourselves. He is now a *damn filthy rich* lawyer, and I have been fired from my job. He's just finished preparing a multimillion-dollar contract, and I was supposed to fly from south-east Turkey to Istanbul following a book event, but I skipped the connecting flight as soon as I heard about what was happening in Ankara. A second of ridiculous grinning and then he shouts, 'This is a fucking carnival! The real deal!' Another tear-gas attack and he pushes me gently: 'Run, Cinderella, run!' We part, heading down different streets, throwing ourselves carefree into the waves of a human sea, confident the water will take our weight.

Strangers are hugging, kissing, protecting each other. People of all ages are dancing in between the police attacks; the wealthy and the poor are singing with formerly unused parts of their lungs. Now and then I see the surprised faces of young people hearing their own chanting voices for the first time; they are learning to shout loud enough not to be able to hear themselves. The joy of crossing all boundaries and challenging all accumulated fears melts into the big, sweet drunkenness of becoming one, free of our selves. It is a night that erases all knowledge of the evil that lies in human beings, and we suddenly see each other as the source of good, only good, even though we are surrounded by the tear-gas clouds of evil. People are tweeting, 'How beautiful we are!'

Between the gas attacks, whether face-to-face or online, people are coming up with some of the wittiest humour the country has ever witnessed, mocking the powers that be, the sacred cows, the untouchable, the fearful. Someone with the handle 'Allah' is tweeting from up above, 'To all those on the streets tonight: Your place in heaven is guaranteed,' an act of heresy impossible to imagine prior to this night. Danger and pain are collectively challenged and confronted. 'Bring it on!' shouts the crowd after each volley of tear gas. And in the wake of each attack, as the wind thins out the gas, dancing silhouettes reappear and sing, 'It didn't hurt anyway!' Beer glasses are raised, and a carnival anthem is invented on the spot: 'Here's to you, Tayyip!' All the anger that's been choked back throughout the years of oppression seems suddenly to have been swallowed, digested and spat out as laughter, and we savour our new-found strength. We have learned to call the king by his first name, and his throne has become nothing more than a ridiculous high chair.

The crowd seems to speak with a single voice, endlessly cracking jokes, each one stripping away another of life's embellishments, revealing its substance, its simplicity. The laughter is purifying. The ingenuous volleys of mockery are aimed first at the cruel ruler and his hypocritical government, then they move on to

217

every kind of pretentious act. A sense of awe emanates to and from everyone, for the simple reason that we are both the spectacle and the audience. Our bodies magically learn how to operate in accordance with this sudden flood of brother- and sisterhood. The flesh instantly forgets boundaries; personal–public, male–female, young–old, stranger–friend. It's as if we already knew how to act as a single body, and remembered it the moment everybody in unison decided to do so.

Amidst the gas and the smoke I see a mesmerising sight: a young man and woman, probably university students, are trying to hold one of the swans of Swan Park, to protect it from the tear gas. I didn't know it then, but this moment, their determination to protect beauty and elegance in the face of crudity and evil, will inspire my next novel, *The Time of Mute Swans*. More importantly, these events will convince me and many other members of a cynical generation that there might still be an uncontaminated part, a hidden room in the human heart, untouched by notions of hier-archy, power, possession and all the other millennia-old appendages that diminish life's essence and smother its joy. On social media people are sharing their own testi-monies of similar moments of mesmerising goodness: 'I can't believe it. We may die here and yet everybody is so polite and nice to each other.' And to this day I don't know, like others throughout the centuries who have been touched by similar carnivals, whether witnessing

218

such complete humanity, such genuine ecstasy at being alive, was a blessing or a curse.

*'All were deemed equal during the carnival. Here, in the town square, a special form of free and familiar contact reigned among people who were usually divided by the barriers of caste, property, profession, and age.'**

The Russian literary critic Mikhail Bakhtin wrote these words at the end of the 1930s. He was trying to understand what had really happened during the first period of the revolution in Russia, and how the true carnival of revolution had mutated into the sullen organised mass rallies seen under Stalin. Like those of us in Turkey in the summer of 2013, he must have been mesmerised by what he witnessed, and couldn't help but try to prove that the purity of the human spirit had really been there, that it wasn't a fairy tale, that he wasn't merely misremembering. Perhaps as a result of the specific kind of loneliness such memories bring, he felt compelled to go back through the centuries and seek a companion to discuss the matter with. Rabelais, a sixteenth-century French monk, came to his aid with his work *Gargantua and Pantagruel*.

Rabelais was, like Bakhtin, a thinker who had sampled the rebellious laughter of the masses. Bakhtin

---

* Mikhail Bakhtin, trs. Hélène Iswolsky, *Rabelais and His World* (Indiana University Press, 1984).

started analysing the centuries-old text, and wrote *Rabelais and His World* in order to try to understand how this laughter worked, and what it was capable of. Rabelais' work begins with these words: 'When I see grief consume and rot/You, mirth's my theme and tears are not/For laughter is man's proper lot.' And Bakhtin's starts with a quote from Alexander Herzen: 'It would be extremely interesting to write the history of laughter.' These three men, in a sense arm-in-arm, endeavoured to look into the depths of collective laughter, an *all too human* means of expression, and no less wonderful for it. Bakhtin knew that only those who had witnessed carnivalesque resistance could really understand one another, even if they were separated by centuries. And he knew all too well, as anyone who witnessed the joyful resistance movements of the early twenty-first century did, that mass laughter leaves a permanent mark on your soul, even after the resistance falls apart, changing the very fabric of all who participated in it.

Bakhtin's work was not published in the USSR until 1965, for obvious reasons: he was telling the story of an unregulated, and therefore dangerous, sort of joy – one that invented songs by calling kings by their first names. The ingenious Bakhtin tried to decipher this special sort of laughter, *terrorist* to all that is artificial. He looked at the brave jester who provoked power's decorum with barbs, not the *pagliacci* who obediently performed amusing tricks to earn a crust. Which is why he wrote the following: 'Festive folk laughter presents an element of victory not only over supernatural awe, over the sacred, over death; it also means the defeat of power, of earthly kings, of the earthly upper classes, of all that oppresses and restricts.'

Like Bakhtin, the people who have joined the carnivalesque resistance movements of the twenty-first century are still trying to understand where the laughter, that magical transformative tool of resistance, comes from. They search not merely out of intellectual curiosity, but out of obstinate hope of recreating the revolutionary moment again. This is why those who joined Tahrir, Gezi and all the other similar mass protests joke and laugh, immerse themselves in humour as if performing a ritual, a séance to summon the spirit to take hold of the streets again.

'We are the soldiers of Gandalf!'

Someone started the joke, and it caught on. During that summer of 2013, city walls throughout Turkey were daubed with similar declarations. After being labelled by the government as the apparatchiks of a plot, the resisting crowd proclaimed that they were the soldiers of Gandalf, of notorious Turkish porn stars, of Yoda, of ancient folk singers, of the footballer Didier Drogba, and at some point even my name appeared on walls as part of the joke. A generation that was unused to being part of a political organisation came up with a new logic, a rebellious narrative. They never answered back to the ruler by saying no; instead, by employing the absurd and the ridiculous they left the ruler standing on his own on stage, alone with his fury. Yet they were far more organised than many other armies in history; walking, talking, breathing and laughing in flawless rhythm despite the fact that there was no one in command.

No wonder that even today, when asked about those heady days and how they managed to behave in such harmony, people talk about the Gezi Spirit, a spirit that was not unknown to Bakhtin or Rabelais. That spirit was the ultimate rejection of power, for it emerged from a huge communion in which the need for power was mocked, and powerlessness was celebrated by embracing every insult directed at them by the ruler. 'Yes, we are looters!' they said, when Erdoğan called them looters. 'Yes, we are alcoholics, the very worst kind!' they shouted back. 'Yes, we are part of a giant conspiracy!' they cried. 'The aliens organised this plot!' And when one of Erdoğan's consultants claimed that they wanted to assassinate Erdoğan by telekinesis, they responded, 'Yes, we are the masters of telekinesis!'

The strength of spirit was not only a consequence of brilliant humour designed to deride those in power; it also came from the sense of brother- and sisterhood established through a carnival that brought out the best in people. Trust, the one commodity that has become so scarce in the age of plenty, was afforded to anyone by everyone, for free. The carnival's ethics rejected overnight an entire set of values based on aggressive individuality and the need to protect oneself from others.

'Here, take my car keys, I'll come and find you tomorrow.'

This is what I said as I gave my keys to a stranger outside a car park in Beşiktaş before walking the last five kilometres up the hill to Taksim, Gezi Park. It was the morning after my Cinderella night in Ankara, the day thousands left work to join the occupation of the city centre. The roads were blocked, and public transportation was stopped to prevent people from getting to Gezi Park, so we walked. As it was the last neighbourhood in which it was possible to leave cars, there were no parking spaces left in Beşiktaş. After making several fruitless circuits, I saw the warden of a building leaning on his walking stick watching people walk by. I asked him if he'd mind watching my car, he said 'Of course not,' and I gave him my keys. He said, 'Shout a flew slogans for me!' It felt quite normal that summer to fully trust in people. Distrust was an oddity.

In the city centre, the crowd moved like peaceful lava, swaying *andante*. They didn't just occupy the space, they interacted with it, constantly reshaping it. A group was gradually turning into a forum; a forum was dissolving into a dance group; the dance drew more people and blossomed into another forum. A library sprang up, a food donation space for those who never left the park, a medical quarter, a painting course for kids, a veterinary corner for street animals affected by the tear gas, and all the other things people wouldn't ordinarily be able to build after a full night of police attacks. The vibrant sense of peace in the square made one think of children making sandcastles; they built as they dreamed and dreamed as they built, until dreaming and building became one single act.

Laughter was transformed overnight, from the occasional emotional outburst to the constant accompaniment to new daily tasks: making gas masks out of plastic bottles; repairing the barricades; writing placards that said 'Withdraw your soldiers, Tayyip. We're going home to have sex!' Such was the sense of ultimate awakening, the rejection of numbness, that many people, reluctant to miss even a moment of feeling so fully alive, found that their bodies refused to sleep. The flow was constant, on the streets and on social media, guided by the Gezi Spirit. The all-inclusive flow *was* the spirit.

However, what no one knew then, just as the Egyptians in Tahrir Square, the Tunisians in the Kasbah and the Greeks in Syntagma Square did not know, was that once all this activity was over, having seen the human being through the kaleidoscope of carnival, those who'd taken part would find themselves becoming the lonely vagabonds of history. They would soon learn, as Bakhtin did, that for the rest of their lives they would seek out companions with whom to recall those glorious days together, to make sure it really happened, that for a moment in history humans were capable of such good, and their laughter made kings tremble with fear. They did not yet know that they would end up desperately trying to imitate their own revolutionary laughter.

'*V for Vendetta* masks. $4. Wholesale only.'
    '*V for Vendetta* masks. $5. Good condition. Original.'
    '*V for Vendetta* masks …'
In 2018, there are countless advertisements on Turkish websites for the masks that were once a symbol of the Gezi protests. As I scroll down them I think back to those days, to a time when the masks were alive and grinning in the face of fear, not dead relics for sale. But there is someone who remembers those masks more vividly than any of us: President Erdoğan. Right after the coup attempt in July 2016, three summers after the Gezi protests, Erdoğan called his supporters to Taksim Square. He intended to wrestle the space from the ghosts still laughing in Gezi Park. He wanted to show that his people were also capable of creating a spectacle, and like Stalin and others of his ilk, he felt sure the carnival spirit could be conjured up via regulated demonstrations, if they were epic enough in

scale. However, Erdoğan's supporters, who he called 'the guardians of democracy', were acting in the name of power, and therefore incapable of producing spontaneous humour – indeed, they stood paralysed until they were told to make a noise. The poor AKP members were commanded by their leader to remain in the square for days, inadequately mimicking the Gezi protesters, hammering out the 'Tayyip Erdoğan' song, which after a night on the streets sounded torturous. Their versions of the Gezi humour were poor imitations; they merely served to elevate the original. Their mission to reclaim the space was physically accomplished, but the spirit was so obviously lacking that after a few days Erdoğan felt compelled to make a seemingly irrelevant statement: 'We are going to build that barracks [in Taksim Square] whether they want it or not.' He was referring to the fact that the Gezi protests had started because of his plan to restore an Ottoman barracks in Taksim. Apparently the Gezi Spirit still haunted Erdoğan too.

But although the masks that had so terrified the ruler were still circulating, they were now transformed into merchandise, lacking the faces behind them that had given their grin its rebellious meaning. Carnival smiles were tainted by sarcasm, and cynicism had begun to rot away the joy. The spirit had been dissected into a million pieces, each one waiting on standby in solitary confinement, trying to survive, believing that provided it could still laugh and make others laugh on social media, it could be kept alive.

'What good's permitting some prophet of doom/To wipe every smile away?/Life is a cabaret, old chum/So come to the cabaret.'

Being jobless and surrounded by genius jobless artists inspires you to do things you never thought you'd do. It is autumn 2015, and I find myself writing a cabaret script. By then every dissident had ended up out of work and doing something different: actors became singers, academics opened cafés, teachers turned to construction work, and sometimes fell and died on building sites. We were all trying to hang on in there, on the edge of an emotional and financial cliff.

The doom-laden environment had left me convinced that cabaret would be the next big thing. When free thought and artistic creation are hounded out by authoritarianism, people retreat indoors, I told my jobless actor friends. The *flow* of dissident energy had been obstructed, so it would run off into little corners, find hiding places to gather in and survive. Joy is becoming grotesque, I kept saying. And for the first time we realised why cabaret had been such a big thing in Germany when Hitler was on the rise. We were learning how only those who were angry at themselves for retreating and feeling helpless would perform such a circus-like spectacle. A certain kind of deep bitterness had crept into the humour, and the jesters who had once been touched by the carnival spirit were now turning on each other. In the end our cabaret never happened, but instead we saw a wicked sort of cabaret being staged wherever the embittered spirit lurked. The Gezi Spirit was damaged, angry and demanding sacrifice via *her dark materials*, the humour that had been discovered during the carnival.

'These hipsters. My God, they don't know how to fight back, do they?'

On 17 June 2016, three summers after the Gezi protests, footage circulated on social media of a young man bleeding severely. Three men from a neighbouring, conservative district had attacked a record shop in the liberal Cihangir district of Istanbul, wielding sticks and threatening to burn people alive. The record shop attack, which left two people, one of them the bleeding hipster in the photograph, seriously injured, was organised for the simple reason that a very small group of young people had been listening to music and drinking a little booze during the holy month of Ramadan. The attackers were released after giving a brief statement, and the owner of the building evicted the little record shop. Residents of the district took to the streets to protest against the incident. But during the night, numerous bitter jokes were circulated on social media referring to the attack, and how the victims were too soft to stand up to their attackers. The references and the style of humour were reminiscent of the Gezi protests, but this time the jokes were sour with sarcasm and ridicule, lacking any hint of the compassion that had been ever-present then. In contrast to the days of Gezi, people were reluctant to associate themselves with the victims, and laughed *at*, not *with*, them. They weren't celebrating or embracing being powerless any more.

Three years after the resistance's retreat, it was unclear whether people were rejecting being a victim or denying that they were one themselves, a victim by association. The dramatic distance between rejecting victimhood and denying it seemed to have been forgotten. And thanks to the effects of sarcasm, the difference between the well and the badly intended blurred, and tiny but significant ethical crimes emerged.

As meeting the regime's oppression and violence with sarcastic humour became a habit, and opposing it with resistant laughter became almost an addiction, it became ever more difficult to differentiate between a joyously dignified rejection of victimhood and plain denial. More importantly, the laughter that had been used as a tool to embrace diversity during the Gezi resistance became a tool to destroy and divide dissidents once rebellious activities had been suppressed and the *flow* stopped. Those who were not capable of limitless sarcasm, those who could not find it in themselves to sustain the carnival approach to violent acts, became excluded from the 'we', the resistance. The creeping cynicism at times changed the character of the carnivalesque narrative, and people became too impatient to offer a shoulder to those who were weeping; the tenderfoots (and sometimes even the shoeless Cinderellas) were left behind. After witnessing this disheartening transformation, from all-embracing joy to excluding amusement, it was easy to become a *prophet of doom*.

'Please be careful with this laughter. Pay close attention to why you laugh and how you laugh.'
My dramatic comment hangs in the air in the vast Lincoln Center in New York, and I feel like a killjoy. It is April 2017, four months after Donald Trump took over the presidency, and an audience of three thousand women have been laughing whenever a joke about *the first orange president of the USA* is cracked on stage. Indeed, it's as if the audience gathered for the Women's Summit don't even need a joke to set them off; the mere mention of Trump's name operates like a secret sitcom trigger for canned laughter. So, as one of the opening-night speakers, I have found myself cast as the *prophet of doom*.

I am stammering out things about how much time we wasted in Turkey by reacting to right-wing populism with humour and sarcasm, trying to laugh away our fears, and how it took our political culture down a cul de sac, bringing about a new type of fatalism, one that

230

always has a smiley at the end. 'This is the first stage,' I blabber. 'The next ones are not funny at all. You will just imitate your first laughter over and over again, until it becomes too narrow a shell to shelter your fears.'

But I am premature in my attempt at demanding that Americans fast-forward their way through the time-consuming stages of shock, and this is clearly a desperate move on my part. Because I remember our first stage, when the laughter felt like our arrows and our shield, essential and indispensable, as it does to them now. We felt that if we made enough clever jokes our reality would become harmless, and at times our awe at ourselves for creating such a stupendous amount of witty political humour made the brutal reality of what inspired the jokes insignificant. It's too early for my audience to notice that they're merely mimicking their carnivalesque selves, what they experienced during the mass *flow* on the streets dressed in pink pussy hats. They too, I think, will place laughter and humour at the centre of their protest – until they cannot. Maybe smiling itself will eventually become an act of resistance for them, as it did for us.

'*Look at this. The deputy prime minister just said, "Chastity is of the utmost importance to us. Women should not be seen laughing in public." Ha ha!*'

Here I am, on the Croatian coast with Petra Ljevak, my Croatian publisher and a dear friend. It is the summer of 2014, and for the past hour she has been trying to convince me, in her gentle voice, that I should buy a place in Europe, preferably Zagreb, 'just to be safe, you know, considering your situation in Turkey'. I have been in a *situation* for over a year now, my life in constant crisis. It is one year after Gezi, and the oppression is escalating with vigorous acceleration. My voice shrinks to a murmur as I say how humiliating the idea of running away is. But then she reminds me that my books are being treated as 'evidence' in recent arrests, and are banned from prisons, where several friends of mine currently reside. As I tend to do during depressing conversations, I start scrolling through my Twitter timeline. It's then that I see the deputy PM's ridiculous statement about women laughing, an amazing opportunity to change the subject.

Petra takes a photo of me laughing, and I post it on Twitter, adding an elegant hashtag: #resistlaughter, a reference to the resist hashtags that became renowned during the Gezi protests. In a matter of minutes, first Turkish women, then European women, and eventually countless women all around the world, from Alaska to Australia, are posting their laughing photos. A few hours later we're one of the BBC's top-trending topics, and the next day the international media delights in publishing beautiful images of thousands of women, all looking very happy. We are proud of ourselves, because we can laugh 'against' the ruler – but really there's nothing to laugh about. The number of women killed in Turkey has skyrocketed, the worst figures in the country's history, while our illustrious Erdoğan is playing out his endgame to become the omnipotent president, which should be enough to *wipe every smile away*. Yet, just like the women in New York, we felt that as long as we could still laugh, we could turn our defeat around. But what's the point of laughing when you don't really want to laugh, you're just doing it because some politician says you cannot? To keep on laughing when really you want to cry feels like cutting a Joker smile into your face. Why did we do it, then? It was our desperate attempt to keep the *spirit* alive, and to try to protect what little dignity we had left.

Although contaminated by the bitterness of defeat, political humour and the laughter it generates first and foremost revives a sense of community, and serves as a catalyst to regroup when the masses have been defeated and are faced with their collective weakness. Every sound of laughter is like a light in the darkness, flickering to give the community a sense of 'us', while making 'them', the ruler and his supporters, seem less terrifying. But while it rebuilds the community's confidence, it also creates a virtual distance from reality by putting the crisis at arm's length. The collective laughter creates an illusion of standing firm against the humiliation of the oppressor, and it offers soothing self-deception, a panic room to retreat into in preparation for the serious fight ahead. Piling up critical jokes as if accumulating ammunition helps us manage our anxieties about the future. That's why in times of crisis, when each of us seeks to be cooler than we actually are, the need for laughter emerges before the political humour does, not the other way round. That's why three thousand women in New York could hardly wait for another Trump joke to be cracked so that they could fall into fits of laughter, just as we in Turkey reached for Twitter first thing every morning in that summer of 2013, eager to see the best jokes made overnight, to draw on that indispensable sense of strength.

However, there comes a time when the panic room gets too comfortable to leave, and there is a collective reluctance to step out and face reality. When there is nothing to joke about any more, the reflex to laugh lingers like a wandering orphan, pathetically repeating its memories of those halcyon days when opposition voices still believed in a tomorrow, when things would get serious. Or conversely, the laughter is exhausted and even the cleverest jokes barely generate a broken smile. This is the last stage before sarcasm turns fatalistic and poisons the human mind. This is the phase in which everybody jokes about almost anything, and oppressed voices start turning on each other, and nobody laughs.

* * *

'At least that makes us sexy! We'd make damn good agents provocateurs!'

Our exuberant laughter raises a few eyebrows at Le Pain Quotidien in Covent Garden, London. My Iranian journalist friend and I are clinking our wine glasses like three exclamation marks: Cheers!!! The appropriate punctuation, had we been truly happy. People turn their heads to watch this sequence from a Middle Eastern *noir* movie, as we prolong our laughter of despair. They doubtless don't understand why, after a few minutes, we suddenly both stop and look in different directions, chins in palms, as silent as can be.

It is the end of summer 2013. I am – once again – keeping out of the country, thanks to two telephone calls from well-connected journalist friends who warned me, in the last days of the Gezi protests, not to re-enter the country. My Iranian journalist friend, meanwhile, has been openly threatened by her government for over a year. We are stranded prey in open season, pretending that we just enjoy running. Her government labelled her a 'foreign agent', and the government trolls in Turkey call me a 'provocateur'. And together those two slurs make us a seductive underwear brand, a sexy couple, as it were – which is the last thing you feel like when you're afraid to go home. An erotic Iranian website is posting bedroom stories pretending to be her, making up juicy details, while one of the most prominent government-supporting Turkish journalists wrote a column about me saying that I 'personally master-minded' the Gezi protests, even giving my seat number on my flight to Ankara on the day the protests started there. The only reason we don't cry is that we cannot say a ladylike 'Oh, sorry,' before just wiping away the tears like soap opera stars. So we force the laughter to its limits. After a few sips she asks, 'What's next then?' I imitate my Gezi laughter and say, 'We'll keep on being sexy, luv!' She does not laugh, and asks, 'No seriously, what's next?'

'So what's next?'

In 2001, at Porto Alegre airport in Brazil, I'm sitting with an older man who's taking the same late-night flight to Buenos Aires. When he introduces himself – 'Tom ... Tom Hayden' – his name doesn't ring a bell, and Googling isn't a verb yet, so I don't know he is *the* Tom Hayden, the famous anti-Vietnam War activist, politician, writer, and of course former husband of Jane Fonda. We'd met in the World Social Forum (WSF) pressroom a few days earlier, and this is the second time we'll bump into each other. The third will be a more sombre affair, but for now we talk about carnivalesque opposition, having been mesmerised by the joyful international crowd in Porto Alegre. The countless busy daytime forums, held under the slogan 'Another World is Possible', and the nights of dancing like there's no tomorrow; anti-capitalist movements from all over the world celebrating their very existence after a decade of destructive self-criticism from the global left; people trying to find out how to overcome and move beyond a neoliberal world. The actual neoliberal world, meanwhile, was in Davos, following the WSF via a live feed, anxious to keep an eye on what was happening at the rebellious carnival. After Seattle 1999, the lords of global capital were understandably curious about the next move these clownish new creatures with masks would make.

But neither Seattle nor the WSF marked the beginning of the idea of carnivalesque resistance: 'socialism with a human face' in 1970s Czechoslovakia, the riotous Orange Dwarves of 1980s Poland, and other equally playful European resistance movements paved the way for rethinking political protest, while bringing a warm and humane face to leftist movements after their image became contaminated by the authoritarian regimes of the USSR and the Iron Curtain countries. Michael Hardt and Antonio Negri's *Empire*, published in 2000, which spoke of this new kind of resistance, was a bestseller, and rebellious laughter became the next big thing: resisting with mirth and ridiculing the ruler to bring the untouchables of the neoliberal system down.

After three days of *caipirinhas* in plastic cups and lots of notes bearing coffee stains, I sat in my hotel room the night before travelling to Buenos Aires to report on the economic crisis and the *piquetero* movement, thinking about what would come next. What were we supposed to do when the carnival was over? This was the only hotel I could find in the city, and its rooms were rented by the hour, if you know what I mean. Given all the distracting sounds coming from neighbouring rooms, I struggled to come up with an answer, and soon found myself at the airport sitting next to Tom, the wise old man. So I asked him, 'What's next?' He just smiled. I was too young to know that only those touched by a carnival, as he'd been in the 1970s, acquired such a smile, wordless yet carefully crafted to keep the answer floating in the air, not letting it come to earth, but not letting it disappear into the clouds either.

The next morning in Buenos Aires, I watch as the Mothers of the Plaza de Mayo move like gravestones to their missing children. They are the women whose children 'disappeared' during the state terrorism of the military dictatorship between 1976 and 1983. They began to march in silent protest at the Plaza de Mayo in 1977, and since then they have never stopped. Old women, arm in arm, grind their way into history as they walk in a circular motion around the city's main square. The windows of the presidential palace look down on the square, and the mothers are a reminder that though the politics may change, and presidents come and go, these women will always be there, walking a decades-long walk, while not going anywhere. They are the noble spirits of pain, carrying the country's dignity on their broken backs. I take in their white headscarves, the 1970s sepia headshots of their children, the easy movement of their shoulders, muscle-memory of years of sisterhood, and the dignified way they wear their faces of despair. They remind me of the Saturday Mothers of Turkey, who stood with the same spirit in the heart of Istanbul for two decades.

The resistance of pained mothers all around the world is the opposite of the new carnivalesque resistance celebrated in Porto Alegre. It isn't just impossible to smile in Plaza de Mayo; the atmosphere compels political tourists like myself and Tom Hayden to rally ourselves. As we spot each other at opposite ends of the square our smiles of recognition soon die away. The ritual for visitors is that you walk with the mothers in silence. They don't look at you, or talk to you necessarily, but nevertheless you put your body in the square. And they nod and stare. But I know that there must once have been a time when even these most determined of women had laughter to spare.

'You must try this one. And that one too. But you haven't even had this one yet!'

Fatma, a fifty-five-year-old woman in a little house in the Ankara slums, was encouraging me to eat a whole tableful of food. It was the winter of 1996, both her sons were in jail, and somehow I was supposed to eat their share too. Her boys were nineteen and twenty, and both were on hunger strike. Yet here was Fatma trying to make me eat, and refusing to hide her grin as she attempted to hook me up with the eldest. 'He is one year younger than you, but that's all right,' was her line, which she kept repeating.

I was the twenty-year-old cub reporter constantly writing about the hunger strikes of the political prisoners, most of them around my age or even younger. Fifteen hundred of them were protesting against the newly-built solitary confinement cells with an indefinite hunger strike. Fatma wasn't the only mother who joked about me marrying one of her slowly dying sons. This inside joke, always cracked when the men weren't around, became one of the little hooks that stopped the women from falling off the cliff into a sea of pain, and it was being with them that taught me how to do forced laughter. Even when two of the parents of the political prisoners started their own hunger strike in solidarity in the Human Rights Centre, the occasional jokes about 'the bride-to-be' were still there.

Their hard-earned mastery of this specific kind of humour taught me about life's textures: that humans need humour to soften the pain; that laughter is the glue that can keep a shattered life together. Every time the mothers demonstrated in front of the Ministry of Justice and were beaten by the police, the best jokes were cracked when they arrived back at the Centre afterwards, wincing with pain, but laughing at themselves. They laughed at the strange lives they had come to lead, forced out of their kitchens to become old-age *terrorists*. But when the first of what would become twelve deaths was reported from the prison, nobody tried to dilute the pain. Then it was just the single and unceasing cry of the mother of the dead prisoner, and the rest of them remained respectfully silent. It was the same silent respect that would fall upon Tom Hayden and me, fresh from the din of the carnival, in Plaza de Mayo five years later.

Resisting through pain exists in a completely different universe to carnivalesque rebellion. Some might even find it boring. However, as opposed to the previous day's playful WSF resistance, for the Plaza de Mayo Mothers the content of their resistance – their goals and demands – was concrete and fully formed. For them the answer to the question 'What's next?' was clear and unchanging, unlike at the WSF and all the other carnivalesque political actions that followed, where the content was blurred by joyous noise. And today, many years after Porto Alegre, when we danced to all that the carnival promised and joined in the addictive laughter, the answer to the same question is still vague and up in the air.

'And Jeremy Corbyn will be releasing his new single. I'm particularly interested in that.'

On 16 June 2018, Owen Jones, the young star of Britain's Labour supporters, seemed quite the professional entertainer on stage at the party's music festival, Labour Live – dubbed 'JezFest' by the press. Being a *Guardian* columnist and a vocal Labour activist, he has an Instagram account where he posts lovely photos of his cat and fun videos that invite his followers to embrace Labour's political line or to attend party demonstrations. He belongs to a generation that has been trying to add fun to politics, until politics and fun become the same thing. However, despite the fact that the Brits are a fun-loving people – at least for a few limited hours on weekends – the one-day festival was not exactly a riot. According to several newspaper observers it was a reluctant fun day rather than something truly carnivalesque. The reason may well have been, I thought, that people are tired of the endless entertainment that politics has been expected to be in recent decades, and of the fact that our politicians have become performers. Also, the carnivalesque cannot be regulated, ticketed and enacted from a stage that separates the audience from the spectacle. The fun that was imposed on the politics that day was not in accordance with the texture of life.

Ironically, on the same day in Turkey, Muharrem İnce, the social democrat candidate who represented our last hope for the country, was campaigning for the coming election, and not unlike Corbyn and Jones, felt compelled to make the crowd laugh and enjoy themselves. As he had done several times during the campaign, he performed a folk dance on the rally's big stage. While watching similar scenes unfold in British and Turkish politics, and as someone who had, after witnessing the joy of Porto Alegre, argued in favour of injecting a little laughter into the political discourse, I couldn't help but wonder: are we pushing the idea of the carnival too far, and turning everything into entertainment?

Around the same time that regulated festivals of social democracy were taking place in Britain and Turkey, President Trump was meeting Kim Jong-un in Singapore to discuss nuclear weapons. Although things couldn't get more serious than this, Trump was busy joking with photojournalists: 'Getting a good picture, everybody? So we look nice and handsome and thin? Perfect.' Not being a slender man, Kim's facial expression suggested he was far from amused. Apparently, despite the fact that the topic of the day was nuclear obliteration, Trump intended to approach international politics like a WWE wrestling bout, a bizarre form of entertainment that is among America's contributions to the global understanding of fun. He was merely replicating wrestling's formula of creating caricatured characters to entertain the audience. Trump was 'the Very Perfect President', challenging 'the Chubby Asian Tiger' to get in the ring. But as there is surely no doubt that when it comes to entertainment no leader can match

Trump's skills, why are leftist politicians trying to beat their opponents at their own game?

How long can we stretch out the fun before getting down to the heart of the matter? How long can we sugarcoat the nitty-gritty of politics in order to draw the apolitical masses to the carnival? And when we finally do get to the heart of the matter, how many festival-goers will stay alongside the activists for the boring bit? Or are we supposed to hold our smiles indefinitely, and leave the answer forever hanging in the air? More importantly, is the answer really that obscure, or are we just afraid of talking about it, in case it clears the dance floor? Are we afraid of the fact that the answer will probably divide the masses that we've only just lured to the party and strung along with carnival spirit? After two decades of humour, laughter, music and dance, aren't we done yet?

This global scene of carnivalesque resistance reminds me of a nature documentary I once saw. Three baby cheetahs take their first steps in learning how to hunt from their mother. Unfortunately for them, their mother dies after they've learned how to catch their prey, but before they've been taught how to kill it. Left to their own devices, they realise they have to feed themselves, and go hunting. However, every time they catch something they put their paws on it, stop, wait, and look at each other. As they don't know the next step, they start playing with their catch, until eventually it escapes. In the end they all starve to death. I never understood why the documentary-makers didn't help the dying animals.

As we all found out after the carnivals of resistance in Tahrir, Gezi and elsewhere, laughter exposed the fact that our rulers' thrones were just ridiculous high chairs, but that wasn't enough to bring them crashing down. The joyous spirit didn't point in any direction after leading people into the squares. The answer lay in neither the laughter nor the carnival venue. What we were supposed to do once we got our paws on the prey remained elusive. So we kept on playing until the prey escaped. Still we crave the juicy flesh of an answer.

Yet in recent years there have been some instances of baby cheetahs learning on their own to bite that amorphous beast, the establishment. In the United States the new rising stars of politics are emerging from the democratic socialists who have accelerated their movement towards visibility, fuelled by the political behavioural culture of the Occupy movement and the urgency generated by Trump's presidency. However, these young heroes and stars are still struggling to find a footing inside the Democratic Party establishment. Greece and Spain are currently the only countries where the carnivalesque resistance movements have established a presence within the conventional venue of national politics, and are able to have a say in the decision-making process. It remains unclear, though, whether this is a forward evolution towards a new kind of politics, or in fact a domesticating type of retreat back to the old forms of representative democracy. It seems the two-way flow between conventional politics and new politics that emerges in carnival resistance – both of them learning from each other on equal terms and changing each other in harmony – has yet to be successfully recreated within the big boys' league of representative democracy and party politics. Those who once savoured the carnival in the open-air *agora* are not satisfied by the staid indoor conversations of the *senate*, but they are also not yet powerful or present enough to change it to match their imaginations.

I remember the last days of the carnivals of resistance in Istanbul and Cairo. The carnivals were exhausting themselves, but were trying hard to keep the spirit as vigorous as it had been in the first few days. People were like laboured actors in an amphitheatre, improvising jokes to gain time until the lead actor arrived; a merciful documentary-maker, so to speak. What they were supposed to do if the soldiers and police didn't violently attack them remained a mystery. The multitude was unable to carry the *flow* into the realm of real politics. I remember an exhausted young man in Tahrir who remained in the square after the big crowds had left. I asked him why he was still there. 'I can't leave,' he said. 'I don't know where to go.' Another young Tunisian man, who looked strangely like his Egyptian comrade, once told me that after he was swept away from the Kasbah, where the Tunisian resistance took place, he couldn't stop drinking. 'Because everything seems … I don't know … incomplete,' he murmured. And whenever I drink with friends from Turkey, when we force ourselves to somehow have fun, our Gezi stories always crop up, followed swiftly by our expressions of hopelessness about party politics. We are the compatriots of a shapeless political *Multitude** craving an answer. This multitude is still too young to decide what to do with itself, but is too old simply to play in the sandpit and daydream. Its adolescent body, at times clumsy but at other times brilliant, keeps on trying, searching for a route to follow the flow. And the more it craves the answer, the more it dances – to pass the time.

'Because they are now in the last phase – the dancing phase.'

As the Anatolian folk story goes, the merciless sultan puts taxes up. Every time the tax collector goes to the village, the poor villagers beg him to spare them. But

---

* See Michael Hardt and Antonio Negri, *Multitude: War and Democracy in the Age of Empire* (Hamish Hamilton, 2005).

instead, taxes are put up again. The villagers starve, and cry more and more on every visit, but the tax collector is unmoved. However, one day he arrives and sees the villagers are all dancing. He reports back to the sultan, 'We have to stop the tax rises, my lord.' The sultan asks why. 'Because,' the collector says, 'they are now in the dancing phase.'

One of the most popular witty lines on social media a few years after the Gezi uprising was 'Go insane if you have the means.' People were posting footage of a variety of crazy people, and begging to go insane themselves, so as not to feel anything any more. 'The dancing phase,' people were saying. 'I want to reach it right away.' They were not so much objecting to oppression, as to the barrage of absurdity that accompanied it. The pain of being subjected to barefaced evil is one thing, but it's quite another to have oppression projected as 'true democracy', as the will of the *real people*; to bear witness to political power doing one thing while claiming to do the exact opposite.

When children by the dozens are repeatedly raped at a hostel run by a pro-government Islamist foundation in Karaman – a conservative town and the stronghold of the governing party in 2016 – and when the journalists who report it, instead of the perpetrators, are jailed; when members of the government then praise the foundation as the most conscientious institution in the country in terms of children's rights, and arrange

a family photoshoot with the foundation's representatives – what possible response is there? Your mouth
falls open wide with shock, you're rendered speechless,
your eyes bulge, and a sound like a hiccup pops out
of your mouth: 'Ah!' And your brain, deceived by the
tension in the facial muscles, starts producing laughter.
This is the laughter that occurs at humanity's emotional
limits. When the mind is forced to test its capacity for
processing the repulsive and the illogical, and when
the size of that task expands and becomes ever more
frequent, until it is utterly relentless, the brain simply
ends up overloaded, and thus it delivers an error
message. It's as if this new type of emotion is unable
to find its place on the map of neurons, and can only
emerge as laughter. This happens when you run out of
anger, and when your supplies of despair and disgust
are exhausted too. And unlike the sultan in the folk
story, the ruler keeps on pushing the limits further and
further, until the repulsive and the absurd become the
new normal.

'Americans want strong borders. Trump has got to stay
tough on this, and ignore the screams coming from the
liberal media,' said Nigel Farage on 20 June 2018. The
issue in question was the 2,300 immigrant children
separated from their parents and put in 'tender age
shelters' due to the US administration's 'zero tolerance'
policy at its Mexican border. Trump, meanwhile, in

response to questions like, 'Mr President, don't you have kids yourself?', was busy declaring that immigrants wouldn't be allowed to 'infest' the US.

Anyone in Turkey watching reports of the crisis would have remembered an expression that became famous under Erdoğan: 'You are so evil it's as if you were never a child yourself.' Doubtless Rachel Maddow, a commentator on MSNBC, was thinking much the same when she choked up with anger and disgust while trying to read out the breaking news story. Perhaps she didn't realise it yet, but she was passing the last exit before the dancing phase. In this phase, after swallowing her disgust and shock, she then had to endure the government's supporters making fun of her tears, before watching as the White House issued a statement saying that no government had ever been as sensitive to children's rights as the Trump administration.

Now imagine this happening every other day for years. That's when the 'Ah!' comes out, followed by the laughter of insanity. This is nothing like the smirk triggered by sophisticated gallows humour, such as that produced by Brits after the Brexit vote. Between that first reaction of laughing to keep your sanity, and the final one that's a product of a human mind damaged by the maddening frequency of anger and despair, there is a period of acute suffering. So when the insanity arrives, it feels like relief, a wicked sort of fun. But in order to truly savour it you have to join the brotherhood of the helpless and the spent, to become high on fury. Then you too can dance the dance of insanity, that halfway house between catatonia and drooping, a dance that is devoid of spirit but wears a fixed grin, a hollow mask that was once used in a carnival.

SEVEN

Build Your Own Country

'*My daughter's teacher assigned her* The Encyclopedia of Non-Existent Birds *by Ece Temelkuran for summer reading.*'

On 25 June 2018, the day after what felt like the 'last hope' presidential election in Turkey, there was a strange and unprecedented silence. Following spectacular opposition rallies, a chorus of discontent voiced by all political parties united against authoritarianism, and a countrywide web of volunteers vigilantly protecting against election fraud, it was suddenly like the last scene of *Gladiator*. Wounded Maximus was making his final stand against the psychotic emperor, and the audience held its breath. The entire body politic was ready to jump into the ring at the first sign of dirty tricks from the emperor, which were only to be expected. They were all waiting for a signal from the hero during the vote counting. But our Maximus, Muharrem İnce, the leader of the main opposition party who had stirred up an unprecedented sense of rebellion in the country during the election campaign, ended up acknowledging, before all the votes had even been counted, that Erdoğan had won yet another victory. 'Well, he won. This is how democracy works,' İnce said, sounding like a footballer who doesn't want to complain about either the biased referee or his broken leg.

Actually, this is definitely *not* how democracy works, and for many of us it had been tragically clear for quite some time that it no longer worked, full stop. The celebratory gunshots of government supporters out on the streets were an apt evocation of what kind of country awaited everyone else from then on. Large sections of the Turkish population felt convinced that they had lost their country and, one way or another, prepared themselves to feel homeless, either in a foreign land or within their own borders. Meanwhile, I sat staring at a dark playground behind my apartment in Zagreb, smiling.

Lately, being a writer has become as much about talking as it is about writing. Thus I am compelled by my profession, and especially on historic days such as a last-chance election, to don layers of Christian Dior *poudre* and use all my political theory books to adjust the height of my computer screen in order to give Skype interviews. On the evening of 25 June 2018, after talking to BBC World News, Euronews, Channel 4 News and several international radio stations, and having written an article about the election for the *Guardian*, I was left sitting there in my smudged intellectual make-up, alone in my apartment in a country that was not my own. Once again it was time for me to retreat to the edges after looking at my homeland through the lens of the 'political commentator'. War photographers and cameramen and women talk about how they come to rely on the illusion of the 'machine': as long as their eyes are locked onto the viewfinder, they can believe that the bombs and bullets won't touch them. The craft of writing performs a similar mental trick by keeping reality at arm's length. Some may call it courage, but actually it is the illusion we cling to that nothing will happen to us as long as we write – and, of course, are read. But once the job is done, the illusion disappears.

And so, like the Little Prince sitting next to his rose on a distant planet, that night I found myself smiling at an insignificant sentence on Twitter as it blossomed. A young mother must have posted it from somewhere in Turkey: '*My daughter's teacher assigned her ...*' In my mind's eye, the girl was growing up, meeting a boy – let's say a boy with a merciless, beautiful smile – and while she nervously talked about herself, seeking a common interest that would be a sign they were meant for each other, *The Encyclopedia of Non-Existent Birds* would come up. The boy, nonchalantly playing with his hair – ah, that sly old trick! – would say, 'Oh yes, I remember that one,' and they would laugh at the silly book they both once read. How magical would that be, right?

This is what happens when things go really wrong in your homeland. When there is no longer a *we* to stand for a reality experienced together, *I* can only retreat to the island of magical imagination; a land of fairy tales with non-existent birds flying over it.

While writing this book I have meticulously followed, every day throughout 2017 and 2018, the ugliest representations of humankind and politics. I was also required to syphon back up all the political and emotional spillage that had left my soul, and the souls of my fellow citizens, bone dry, in order to alert others who are soon likely to find themselves on the road to losing their country. In the spring of 2018, after finishing the second chapter, when I felt as though I'd had my fill of all that is ugly and banal in the world, one early morning, like a child grabbing her crayons as soon as she wakes up, I began to imagine a bird, of a non-existent breed. Every dawn that followed, I would wake up and create another bird, immersing myself in this fantasy book. I made up superstitions about imaginary birds in Scandinavia, wrote old Mongolian folk songs for others, even established rules for a certain style of ancient wrestling in China inspired by a fantastical duck. With their made-up Latin names my collection of birds became a book that would go on to be published in Turkish, my mother tongue. I wanted to send beautiful things to fly back home, like a poet carving her name on floating logs in a river to inform people far downstream that she is still alive in Siberia. The idea was as silly as flying a kite during an air raid to remind the victims that the sky is bigger than the bombs. But it was the only thing the fragile pronoun *I* could think to do. Buried in that book were my fears that my country would one day become an entirely strange land, and my hopes that I would not end up as a total stranger to the next generation, one that would be born into my mother tongue but 'not my country'.

After all, it was far more likely that our ruler was already done with the present, and that the future would be sprayed with the Agent Orange of authoritarianism to ensure the land remained barren for generations for strange birds like me.

'God damn these people!'
Kids are parading through the streets of a commercial district in Istanbul. They must be aged between eight and twelve. Boys in the front are wearing *taqiyah*, a short, rounded Islamic skullcap. The girls, all in pink headscarves, are at the back, for ultra-conservative

Islamist women must walk behind their men. There is a Janissary band marching at the head of the procession, and the placard the kids are carrying reads 'The Summer Quran Course is Starting'.

This video circulated on social media the day after the historic election. The man filming it on his smartphone spoke in the low voice of the defeated. 'Look at this,' he said. 'Poor kids. They should be playing at this age.' Then he directed his camera at the Quranic teachers guarding the children; covered women for the girls and men wearing *taqiyah* for the boys. He murmured again. 'God damn these people!' The children were as happy as newborn tigers in a circus cage.

The footage was a vivid confirmation of the fact that we were now expected to live in a country where the next generation would have very different references and common codes from the ones we had, a country that would most likely exclude anyone who did not comply with the norm. 'A new generation that would hold on to its religion and grudges' was being built, just as President Erdoğan had promised years ago. But there were still a few who were determined enough to say, 'We should also build our own education system. We should at the very least protect the next generation.' For beneath the prevailing sense of surrender there remained a resolve to struggle for the future. That was why I had smiled at the tweet in my apartment in Zagreb, at a girl who, in my mind's eye, might grow up to be a bit like me: another strange bird who just might remember me.

'This is not my country!'

So shouted a woman in the USA in the last days of June 2018. She was voicing the sentiments of many while speaking to a reporter about how cruel it was to separate children from their immigrant parents as part of Trump's zero-tolerance border policy. Thousands of people across several cities rejected being part of an America where immigrant toddlers were expected to appear in court alone. A five-year-old was crawling on the table in a courtroom, and a girl too young to know which country she was from was trying to draw it with crayons for her lawyer. Movie star Susan Sarandon was in police custody with another five hundred people for occupying a state office in protest at the ridiculous cruelty, and Trump supporters were trashing her for being an 'attention whore'. It was *their* country now. *They* were taking it back from the 'elite', while Trump was busy saying, 'They call themselves elites. We *are* the elites. We are the super elites!' The *real people*, who had become the *super elites* within the space of a year, were all for separating children from their parents in order to make America great again, while their fellow countrymen and women were determined to at least try to protect others from what they couldn't protect themselves from. The hesitant question – 'Is this my country?' – which they had been asking themselves for the past year, had already begun its retreat, replaced by a despairing 'This is not my country.'

'What is a country? While searching for an answer to this question, I recalled the great Theo Angelopoulos movie. "What is tomorrow?" the film asked, and the answer was the title, Eternity and a Day. *A country, I thought, is in fact a vast land and a table. It is a table surrounded by loved ones to whom you don't have to explain your jokes, and the vast land that surrounds it, which is mostly your imagination.'*

It was 2011 when I wrote this, on a day that I still remember vividly. I was standing at a gate in Tunis airport after talking to my lawyer, who had said, 'They're arresting journalists by the dozen today. Take a vacation or something. I don't know, go away some-where.' I looked at the passengers boarding the plane to Istanbul, then down at my boarding pass. While trying to change my ticket from home to *somewhere else*, it was the first time I felt that Turkey was hardly my country. *My* country was actually a table, not the vast land that surrounded it. A table that I owned. The land around it had disowned me – or at least it convinced me that it had at the time.

*   *   *

The vast land you thought you belonged to does not shrink down to a table overnight. It takes years. You may assume that the cause of this shrinking is oppression and the fear it generates. But in fact it does not begin at the moment a clown takes over the presidency, or a psychotic emperor starts barking orders at the nation from his palace. It does not start when biased laws are enforced against dissidents as if they're prisoners of war, or when being punished by the law ceases to feel like the understandable consequence of your actions, but instead like unlawful revenge meted out by an enemy. It does not even begin the moment you realise that unprecedented breaks with justice have become routine. Looking back, it becomes clear that the process only really starts after severe damage has been wreaked to the fundamental concept of justice, and once the minimal morality you didn't know you depended on has been destroyed. It is this exhausting, terrifying immorality that forces you to look for a *somewhere else*. It is not the emperor who pushes you to the edge of the arena to become merely a disassociated observer, but his subjects.

'Run! Run! It's on the other floor!'
    Ambassadors, parliamentarians, journalists: there are more than fifty of us in total, and we are running from floor to floor in the gigantic Palace of Justice in Istanbul. It is 2010, and this is the new technique of

ridiculing the opposition in courtrooms. Whenever
there is a political case that is monitored by dissidents,
like this one today, we are first told to wait outside
a particular courtroom, and then, at the last minute,
they change it so that all those attending, many of them
middle-aged, have to run to a different floor. And then
they do it again, and we run again. Most of the crowd
end up gasping for breath, and when we finally find
the mystery courtroom it turns out to be the smallest
one in the whole building, so even if we squeeze in like
sardines, many still end up stranded outside.

More often than not, the hearing will be the first time
we have seen our imprisoned friend in over a year, for he
or she will have been held in a prison cell without a court
hearing through all that time. Meanwhile, the prosecutor laughs at the panting observers, and sometimes the
judge throws out anyone who takes exception to being
the butt of this particular joke in the so-called 'Palace
of Justice'. (When the concept is destroyed, they build
palaces out of it instead, apparently.) Since the mainstream Turkish media does not report on their trials,
nobody knows what's really going on with thousands
of political prisoners, so our job as witnesses is also to
live tweet about the case: tweets that some of us translate into English for the rest of the world to understand.

When the hearing finishes, we go out to meet the few,
by-now exhausted, members of the opposition press.
We know them all, they all know us – we could all fit

around a single table, in fact. They have all been, or are still being, sued themselves, and many have been defendants at similar trials to the one we're witnessing today. The police, who far outnumber us and our colleagues, stare at us, waiting to pounce on any detail in the press statements that oversteps the mark so they can start harrying us away. But harried or not, we all go home ready to repeat the same thing in a few days' time.

Every once in a while the judge decides to release the defendant, and those attending hug each other. They always tweet the same thing: 'We rescued our friend from their clutches!' But then we start to think, did we really? Or do the judges just periodically release some of the detained in order to take some of the heat out of the situation? And while we're asking ourselves these questions, it is not at all uncommon for the released person to be arrested again on new charges as soon as they leave the courthouse. So the tweets are refreshed: 'We are going to rescue our friend from their clutches!' This in turn is met with mockery: 'See how they start running again!' And we are left to wonder, is everyone mocking us? Are we just part of a huge, horrible joke in which our suffering provides the comic material?

We no longer live in the world of Spartacus, Gandhi, Nelson Mandela or Bobby Sands, where the dignity of those suffering is recognised and the determination of their struggle eventually forces onlookers to intervene in the name of humanity. Our world is one where those who resist are mocked as 'attention whores', and where there is no longer the possibility of a noble martyr's death for those who are oppressed, instead only the likelihood of violation and disfigurement by internet trolls. The victim is not even labelled an 'enemy of the people', which one might at least wear as a badge of honour under a dictatorship, but is instead turned into a public joke.

This is not the classic story of the ruler discrediting dissident public figures through his propaganda machine; it is much more bleak than that. It is as though, when the fallen gladiator tries to fight back against the cruel emperor, the Romans, *en masse*, begin to joke about how chubby Russell Crowe looks as he's dying. And someone will, of course, take a selfie with the fallen warrior and post it online with a cheerful emoji. Or cut and paste some video clips to create a short *Borat*-like mockumentary turning the victim into a laughing stock as the little *artwork* goes viral. The age of pretending not to see the victim is over. This is the era of gawping at the oppressed and having a good laugh about it, even when the oppressor hasn't actually called for you to do so.

*   *   *

The struggle for freedom and dignity has become a reality TV show, and is no longer a battlefield on which the Geneva Conventions' rulings on the treatment of prisoners of war have any validity. Perhaps for the first time in human history, the dirty and disgusting comic material that discredits the oppressed is being produced not by the ruler, but by the audience, acting out of their supposed free will. And those who try to hold on to their sanity and morals during this process, and to stand in solidarity with the oppressed, not only have to share in their hardship, but also in the shame of being mocked, and its silencing effect.

Bringing actions and bodies together, as we did in our carnivalesque protests, is becoming harder and harder, not so much because of oppression, but because of the paralysing fear of being shamed and mocked. Because it is not the death or rape threats, or the fact that thousands of people make you into a target, a 'traitor' who's next in line to be imprisoned, that get to you, so much as the ridicule. At a certain point, even death threats seem to have a little bit of class compared to the mockery, which strips you of all dignity. Somewhere along the way you come to the bizarre realisation that while you can proudly show people the death and rape threats, when it comes to the mockery you are ashamed to share it even with your friends, because there is always the chance that one or two of them won't be able to suppress a chuckle, and that would kill you faster than any death threat.

Now imagine being mocked and dismissed in this manner for years on end, and you might understand why 'Is this still my country?' eventually, and for the most part secretly, leads on to 'Is there a place – *I don't know, somewhere, anywhere* – I can go to escape this?'

On 7 July 2018 I was *somewhere*, a little village on the Croatian coast. That night Croatia played Russia in the quarter-finals of the football World Cup, and won on penalties. The priest rang the church bells when the winning penalty was scored; Croatia were in the semi-finals. Croatians look like elves from *The Lord of the Rings* – they are gracefully big. Aware of the spatial mass they occupy, they behave responsibly, even when they are crazy happy. So that night was peacefully victorious. The next morning, one or two cars honked as they drove along the seafront, and some of those who were swimming stopped and waved at them, raising fists of victory, saluting each other. Their country had won, and so, on 8 July 2018, even though these people had never met before, they all felt that they knew each other. For them, on that day, the vast land was like an endless table at which you didn't have to know each other to laugh together.

But there were two people in the village who couldn't share in the joy. An English couple had joined the Brexodus and come to live a secluded life on the Croatian coast, and now they were desperately trying to avoid the only two cafés in the village. Croatia would play England in the semi-finals, and the couple had suddenly become embarrassingly popular. Whenever they passed the big café in the square the locals would salute them in broken English: 'See you on Wednesday, no?! The match! The match!' Every time, the couple had to assure the locals that they'd be watching the match in the café where the entire village was set to gather, to face off against the two of them. They had already reached the mid-July tan limit of their pale skin, but for several days there was no hiding their very British sense of embarrassment as they blushed bright red. They were just two of thousands of Brits who had left their homeland to join 'This is not my country any more' land, a fluctuating, non-specific place with an increasingly mixed population of different nationalities. And that summer they were experiencing, as generations before them had done, the fact that 'my country' can become an even bigger burden when you're not in it, when you're a stranger in someone else's land.

On the night of the match I went to the café, more to watch the English couple than the game. They didn't show up; their reserved table lay empty, surrounded by a foreign land. Perhaps they'd already learned that they'd have to smile the same smile whether England won or lost, because as a stranger one learns very fast always to smile the apologetic tourist smile. I became aware of this smile when I first moved to Zagreb in

2016, and now, apparently, it was their turn to experience the ache in their cheek muscles.

England lost to Croatia that night. The villagers were too happy to remember the English couple. They were not even a joke, too insignificant even to be the subject of mockery.

Today, there are many people who find themselves saying, 'This is not my country any more': in the USA, Hungary, Poland, Germany, Great Britain, and many other places besides. They have become familiar with the feeling of standing still but sensing that the land has moved under your feet. It is as though the master plan for your country has changed overnight, and you are no longer required to help carry it out. What few people realise, however, is how, from the moment it is uttered, that sentence – 'This is not my country any more' – transforms not just the individual who says it, but also their country. The story of what happens to people when they leave their home and become strangers in a strange land has been told many times (maybe more than enough times), but what happens to a *country* when its citizens leave is never discussed. It is as if the country is considered inviolable unless the territory itself is torn apart. This elusive question would have resonated with Iranians, Afghanis and Iraqis some decades ago, and today it speaks to nations that once considered themselves immune to such madness: Britain, America, Germany.

Towards the end of October 2015, the journalist Helmut Schümann asked, in an article for *Der Tagesspiegel*: 'Is this still our country?' He was reacting to levels of xenophobia that were unprecedented in Germany in recent times. A few days later, while he was walking down a street in Berlin, someone approached him, asked him if he was 'that leftist pig Helmut Schümann', and punched him. Appalled by this incident and by similar symptoms of political madness, the opinion editor of *Der Spiegel*, Markus Feldenkirchen, repeated the same question in his column a month later. The way the two German journalists were feeling was not so different from the way we Turkish journalists have been feeling for the last two decades.

When a country turns hostile towards its children, the price an individual can end up paying, whether they leave their country or not, is a bloody lesson that humanity has learned over the centuries, especially in the decades following World War II. But the price the country pays when it is abandoned seems an incalculable equation. The answer is often explored in literature, which can do the 'sliding-doors' trick and reimagine different outcomes for historical events. But even without the help of literature, it is clear that the story, and therefore the soul, of a country is changed irrevocably when it disowns its own citizens.

* * *

'You're talking about Sivas as if it were Paris. Well it's not, to say the least.'

It's 2007, and I am talking to an Armenian PhD student in a café at Harvard University. He is a brilliant young man who naturally keeps up with world affairs and knows about history. However, as he talks about his ancestral hometown of Sivas, a place he has never actually been to, and lavishes it with limitless praise, I find it impossible not to interrupt and ask, 'You do know that Sivas is famous for a massacre, don't you?'

Sivas is a provincial, conservative city in central Anatolia, which appears alongside the word 'massacre' if you Google it. In July 1993, ultra-conservatives there burned to death a group of thirty-five writers, poets and musicians in a hotel for being 'heretics'. A kebab shop subsequently opened next door to the hotel, meaning that annual commemoration ceremonies must be held amidst the smoke of cooking meat. The lawyers who defended the perpetrators, portraying them as sensitive religious people who were provoked, became AKP officials in later years. So it was impossible not to react with sarcasm when the young PhD student waxed lyrical about Sivas, impossible not to say, 'Sivas is not Paris, to say the least.' Quite unexpectedly, and despite his laid-back American accent, a very Anatolian smile of sarcasm appeared on his face as he replied, 'Well, maybe if you'd protected the Armenians in 1915 rather than abandoned us, that massacre might not have happened. If we Armenians still lived in Turkey, who knows, maybe Sivas *would* have become Paris.'

A supposition that I cannot dare to discuss, let alone argue against.

So what would happen if all those people who left their country were to return to their homeland? This question might have sounded fantastical until it was partly answered on 25 June 2018, when thousands of Irish citizens from all around the world travelled home to vote. The referendum to liberalise Ireland's abortion laws gave a generation of Irish women a say on their rights over their own bodies for the first time. As Lauryn Canny, who travelled from LA to vote, told the BBC, the next day Ireland was a 'more compassionate' place. Doubtless that morning many thousands of Irish people around the world were feeling, for the first time in their lives, that they all knew each other; as if they were all seated at the same big table. Many might have felt like saying, '*This* is my country.'

But 'my country' is a compassionate illusion, as much as 'not my country' is a cruel delusion. The country expands in its finest hour, and shrinks on its darkest day. 'Country' is your reality as much as it is your dream, whether it is a burden to be carried in foreign lands, or the weight of feeling like a foreigner in your homeland. It is the history you were taught, or the past that doesn't always make it into the history books, and all the possible and impossible futures you are allowed or not allowed to imagine. A country is too big and too shapeless to be owned completely or disowned entirely. But one thing is for sure: with every departure of a citizen, that individual's past and future are removed from the narrative, and the territory the *gangsters* can invade is enlarged, until it becomes entirely *their* country in the end.

As I am writing this last chapter, Steve Bannon, the former chief strategist to Donald Trump, is embarking on an ambitious – and dangerous – crusade against Europe, in Europe. In several interviews Bannon has said that he is determined to unite the new far right in the old continent to create a global movement, which will divide the European Union. Many people are asking what damage one entitled little man can do to the vast might of Europe, but at the same time – remembering their twentieth-century history – almost all of them also agree that this one-man crusade *could* become dangerous if US dollars start flowing to the European far right. Such ominous news about Bannon and his tempting promise of American cash reminds me of the web of political money that was so carefully woven by Erdoğan and his supporters in Anatolia. Besides, whenever I read an interview with Bannon in which he uses words from the Hollywood lexicon like 'dude', I can't help but imagine him as a new Michael Corleone of politics (apologies to Mr Pacino!), bringing all the mafioso leaders together to form a bigger and stronger clandestine network where they all work alongside each other, until inevitably, in their quest for more power, they start killing one another.

Obviously, this is just my depressing daydream. But recent years have taught us that it might turn out to be real, for other seeming dark fantasies have, without recourse to any dystopian literary device, proved themselves to be so. Our generation is facing – one hopes – the last crisis of neoliberalism, which has forced the ruling system to transform itself into a mafia-style global network. Just as previous generations had to deal with different tricks from the system, we are having to confront the fact that its wobbly set of values can only remain watertight when backed up by virtual and actual weapons of authoritarianism and a systematic manipulation of the masses, often designed to produce hostility. The result is the creation of vast lands of immorality.

Today, almost half the world lives under god-father-like political leaders, and many people genuinely support and vote for them, as in any neighbourhood that has lost all hope of ever getting justice from a crumbling establishment. These leaders are 'their guys', providing some sort of twisted sense of justice, and therefore the neighbourhood obeys their rules without question. That's why all the lavish palaces, all the nepotism, all the misdeeds, all the ruthlessness that you might personally find outrageous and that cause you to say 'This is not my country' are really just the backdrop to the scene they've set out to play. These leaders are the street kids who have learned the ways of court. To the *real people* such leaders are 'our guy in the capital', and if you ask them, they will say that they are no crueller than other leaders, the ones who presented themselves as serious and responsible statesmen, but actually underneath it all were behaving like mafiosi. For many people, these new strongman leaders are their Michael Corleones, who do what they must do to survive in a corrupt world while they try to make it better – or so they would have their neighbourhoods believe. The masses, in growing numbers, therefore end up begging to become the obedient subjects of a palace, a strongman, a godfather.

Once more, we are in a phase of history where the masses are roaring their *sad passions* and *fighting for their servitude as if it were their salvation*, as Spinoza once wrote. These people are not necessarily complete idiots, or deplorables; instead, as many thinkers have found out throughout the course of history, they are normal citizens who, under certain circumstances, circumstances this book has sought to put in some

273

kind of perspective, end up actively seeking authoritarian rulers, and with them, that once out-of-date word, fascism.

It is undoubtedly regrettable that the most evident inheritance our generation has handed over from the rubble of the twentieth century is Vladimir Putin, Marine Le Pen and Tayyip Erdoğan as models of leadership – politicians who every day create thousands of 'This is not my country' people, some of whom are able to leave their land, others who are not. And the rest of the world continues to look on impotently, saying, 'They can't do that. Why would they do such a thing? It's insane!' only for the rulers to carry on regardless, gloating, 'Oh, but we can. And we do it simply because we can.'

This is usually the picture that's painted even by those who wish that things were different. However, in the mafioso plot that's been imposed upon the world today there are several storylines that have still to be finalised. They are, in fact, already changing.

On the right-hand side of the world map, political Islam, having produced millions of 'This is not my country' citizens to scatter around the planet, has lost its prestige and proved itself a fraud of limited imagination and even less viability for the twenty-first century. Wherever they have seized state powers, political Islamists couldn't hide the fact that they were not only incapable of establishing, but also unwilling to establish, the heavenly justice they'd promised. The fake moral high ground of political Islam is therefore being swiftly eroded.

In the middle of the world map, neoliberalism, with its rotting décor of the nation state and representative democracy, lost its cool after millions of Syrians and other migrants spread out into the old continent to test the system's set of values and the limits of this *decorative democracy*. The European Union, an economic giant without a comparable political standing, is coming to terms with the fact that an international body is nothing but an idiotic freak show unless it has moral values it actively defends, and more vital political goals than its mere survival. And the United States is no longer believed by the rest of the world to be an untouchable, omnipotent presence, the phantom that shapes global politics behind the scenes. After repeated failures, its every attempt to enforce some kind of premature democracy in the Middle East looks like the clumsy actions of an adolescent, forever upsetting sensitive political balances that rarely held until the beginning of the twenty-first century. It happened to God, now Superman is dead! Then there is Brexit, of course, the three lions on England's shirt having become three confused kittens just because a referendum was held on a whim. (No, it's no more complicated than that, unfortunately.) A centuries-old arrogance still convinces many that Britain can go it alone, but it is gradually being chipped away, leaving Britain with a more realistic perspective on its place in the world.

Although everything may seem like an insane mess, there are certain realities that are actually clarifying things, helping the many who still resist to write themselves a more humane storyline than a mafia movie, if only they can pull themselves together, shake off their excess emotional baggage and focus on how not to lose their country. For those who have already lost a country, the way not to lose one couldn't be clearer. Our mistake wasn't that we didn't do what we could have done, rather that we didn't know that we should have done it earlier. We were too busy doing what might be called *pseudo-understanding*.

As we did in Turkey, today many people in various countries have been seeking survival by staying *at the edges* of the battle. They observe the messy fight, not realising that they themselves are also supposed to be the gladiators. Our eagerness to *understand* people's 'desire to be slaves' has had us glued to our smartphones and computer screens seeking answers, and the process has become so time-consuming and so fulfilling that we have felt as if things are not actually happening to us. It is not only that we have confused trying to understand with being mesmerised by the ruthlessness of the masses, we have also failed to grasp the fact that understanding requires action. If we are not politically active or reactive, then the act of understanding turns into only the expression and exchange of emotional responses. Our reactions gradually retreat to become nothing more than a sad cabaret. Written or oral expressions of anger and fear replace not only the act of understanding and active conversation, but also actual political action. And as time passes, *I*, the highly capable body, becomes an inadequate pronoun, able only to daydream and to seek comfort in fairy tales, while the new political *we* – the *real people* – become more invasive, and energised with more hostility and manipulativeness. By the end, being at the edge is no longer our *choice*, because in fact there is nowhere else to go.

Today it seems our options are limited. Either we fall into the paralysing emotional loop of 'Is this my country? – This is not my country,' a vicious circle that has no political significance or moral consequence, or else we really understand while acting, and act while understanding. Most importantly, we have to come to terms with the fact that there can be no understanding without action. Otherwise we will soon find there are no uncontaminated edges of the world to retreat to and daydream in.

A human lifetime is tragically disproportionate to humanity's ambitions. We live shorter lives than sea urchins or tortoises, which do not apparently share our desire to create a better world or our capacity to be disappointed when our dreams fall apart. This is perhaps why Samuel Beckett's words seem to have particular resonance nowadays, whenever the opposition fails in a country: 'Ever tried. Ever failed. No matter. Try again. Fail again. Fail better.' He may have been inspired by the nature of sea urchins or tortoises. However, ours is hardly a Sisyphean situation: pushing the rock up the hill once again, or being defeated *better*, is not an option; unlike for previous generations, the world, the air, the sea and the soil are too old now for us to start all over again. Our generation and the next generation will have to answer the question, perhaps for the last time, of how an individual should live and how humanity should conduct itself.

Whatever the answer is, it ought to be clear to all of us that it does not include the luxury of not taking action, namely political action. Our concept of joy should be redefined to understand that collective action does not only make for a better world, but a fulfilled individual. The spontaneous carnivalesque resistance movements were there to remind us of the fact that when you fight your fight it leaves no time for debilitating melancholy to take root. Our generation, and probably the next, will have to find ways to make the joy of uniting sustainable. Otherwise ...

* * *

'We'll talk about this on the island,' said my friend Ayşe. She has a five-year-old daughter, a kindred spirit called Zeyno. Ayşe has been telling me ever since she became a mother that she feels as if she is *performing* for the first time in her life. 'Now I have to be a better person. I'm shaping a human, for God's sake!' she has said repeatedly. And now, as we talk on Skype about the *situation*, she confesses, 'What am I going to tell my daughter when she asks me one day what we did all this time?' Ayşe truly feels ashamed when she says, 'Am I going to tell her, "We tweeted as much as we could"?' I couldn't come up with a good answer, so I said, 'Maybe she won't ask.' In that moment, Zeyno grew up in our minds and turned into a young woman who didn't ask serious questions – and neither of us liked the idea. We frowned at each other and said, 'See you on the island.'

In a few hours I will head to a Greek island, the closest one to Turkey, from where you can see my hometown, Izmir. It is both the nearest to and the furthest from which I get to my country, for you see the land every day, and are reminded that you cannot go back. It is the island where I meet my family and friends and form my table without the vast land that surrounds it. As it has been for a few years, meeting up with them will be an overwhelming experience, like a safari of emotions on my savanna. Away from home, I have learned how to keep my inner birds in order, stable, tamed, seemingly at peace. But when my people, with all their questions and their visible ways of expressing their emotions, enter my internal landscape, bringing joy and the blues, the beasts awaken inside me, they roam, they hide, they become fearful. I understand now why people who live away often look empty and frozen when they meet up with loved ones from back home. It is because after the reunion, *I*, the inadequate pronoun, will have to gather the wild birds back in, calm them down and re-establish serenity. It takes time to go back to the wordless life of the savanna, the only place the birds can rest quiet, at the edge of the world.

This book is my answer to the question I asked in London in 2016: 'What can *I* do for you?' These are the words I can come up with to help you recognise the warning signs that you might be about to lose your own country, and what will happen to *I* when you do. Yet such words ought really to be capable of first evaluating, and then healing, the land I have left behind. There must be a better way than making up silly birds. But those words will not come from *I*, sitting alone *on the edge*, but from *we*, acting together in the middle of the arena, transforming it into a global *agora*.

Acknowledgements

While writing this book several women formed a web that kept me from falling into the abyss of my muteness. Annelies Beck, Mika Buljevic, Petra Ljevak, Mireille Bermann, Merita and Suzanne Arslani, Burçak Ünver, Ayşe Akkızoğlu, Ayşegül Şenarslan, Selen Uçer, Aylin Aslım, Tina Brown, Anna Hall, Kalypso Nicolaidis, Işıl Öz, Şebnem Arsu, Çağıl Kasapoğlu, Hande Yaşargil, my mother Lale Temelkuran, Baroness Beatrice von Rezzori ... There have been many other women in several countries who, sometimes unknowingly, lifted up my soul and helped me to survive over the last two difficult years, mostly the waitresses at the cafés I wrote in. I am thankful to them all.

Thank you Jethro Soutar, for your patience when holding my hand through the infinite plateau of the English language.

Special thanks to my agent Robert Caskie, who heard me, and my editor Helen Garnons-Williams, who saw me.

In order to write this book, although I didn't *kill any darlings* to my knowledge, one of them had to suffer a lot alone. My mentor Demet Börtücene, you will always be the irreplaceable *grande dame* of my life.